THE SEVEN ATTRIBUTES OF HIGHLY COMPETITIVE STAFFING FIRMS

THE SEVEN ATTRIBUTES OF HIGHLY COMPETITIVE STAFFING FIRMS

Jay M. Finkelman, PhD
and
Jonathan Troper, PhD

The Seven Attributes of Highly Competitive Staffing Firms
© 2010 by Jay Finkelman and Jonathan Troper. All rights reserved.

ISBN-10: 0-9774908-4-X
ISBN-13: 978-0-9774908-4-4

Published by:
Crain Communications Inc
1975 W. El Camino Real, Suite 304
Mountain View, CA 94040 USA
(650) 390-6200 (phone)
(650) 390-6210 (fax)
publisher@staffingindustry.com
www.staffingindustry.com

To order bulk copies of this book
Call (800) 950-9496, email booksales@staffingindustry.com or visit the store on our
Web site, www.staffingindustry.com (Single copies are also available at Amazon.com)

Notice of Liability

The contents of this book and the opinions expressed herein represent an interpretation
and analysis of academic research and staffing industry best practices as reviewed by the
authors. Author recommendations may not be appropriate in every situation. Questions
about specific policies or actions for any individual business should be referred to an
attorney, accountant, or other appropriate qualified professional. Neither the publisher
nor the authors are engaged in rendering legal, accounting, or other professional advice
herein. Views expressed by the authors do not necessarily reflect those of the publisher.

Notice of Rights

In loving memory of my parents, Florence and Milton, and to my amazing wife, Princess Maria, our daughter Lauren, and dog Benz.

—*Jay*

To Shmuel Troper, my father, who would have been proud to see this book in print, and to my mother, Judith Troper, who had many interesting experiences as a temporary secretary.

—*Jonathan*

CONTENTS

Foreword

Whether you are just starting out in the staffing industry, have been a long-time staffing business owner, or find yourself moving up the ranks to a branch, area, or regional manager slot, you'll find the insights and advice gathered together in this meaty volume to be highly useful in organizing your thinking about the management and profitability of your business.

Jay Finkelman and Jonathan Troper, both on the faculty at the Marshall Goldsmith School of Management at Alliant International University in Los Angeles, have combined their considerable expertise in organizational psychology and business management with years of hands-on management, teaching and writing experience (much of it in or for the temporary help industry) to offer staffing firm owners and managers the first industry-specific textbook for managing and growing a successful staffing business. Jay brings almost two decades of on-the-job experience at regional and national staffing companies, and Jonathan worked for a couple of years at an executive recruiting firm. They also bring management and management consulting experience from a variety of industries. This book uses real-life situations in staffing firms from the authors' experience to bring theory to life and make the book an enjoyable read.

I predict this work will become a primary handbook for staffing management at thousands of locations in hundreds of industry markets and in dozens of industry segments. I urge staffing owners to make parts of the book required reading for incoming management and again before manager training retreats. While it's probably fair to say that not every staffing executive will find each and every prescription from Finkelman and Troper to their liking, I'll bet most will be delighted overall to hand this book to their corporate and field staff.

Only during the last two decades of the 20th century did staffing services come of age. During that time, many exceptional account, branch and area managers moved from the national companies where they learned the ropes to start up their own successful local, regional and even national staffing businesses. Entrepreneurs of many stripes generally flourished during these times as the penetration rate for temporary help in the U.S. workforce reached two percent, more than double the level of prior years.

As in real estate, the staffing industry of the 1980s and 1990s was particularly hospitable to numerous capable women who were able to build impressive staffing services companies by combining strong relationship-building skills with "street smarts" to land accounts, recruit good workers, and motivate internal staff.

But today, the staffing world, like the rest of business, has become more and more complex, very fast-paced and hyper-competitive. Customers are more sophisticated, and even the most local businesses are often affected by global workforce trends. Technological nuances, savvy risk management practices, sharp change management skills, market segmentation and branding, VOP and VMS positioning, and specialization expertise as well as even stronger leadership and relationship-building skills must now be learned by the successful entrepreneur and, at least to some extent, his or her staff.

Future staffing firm success will also depend on

- reducing internal turnover (still high in our industry) through career development and enhancement,
- further professionalizing the business,
- conquering a growing talent shortage,
- working with multiple business partners and in teams, and
- exploiting the global trend towards independent workers and project employment.

Becoming competitive in these emerging areas will also require a keen command of the management skills outlined herein.

The Seven Attributes of Highly Competitive Staffing Firms will no doubt resonate immediately with a select group of staffing firm owners who are already running their companies with attention to the new business imperatives. They will immediately see the utility of this volume for helping to pass wisdom on down the ranks to develop future leaders. Similarly, upwardly mobile branch and area managers and account executives with aspirations to move up the corporate chart — or perhaps build a staffing business of their own some time in the not too distant future — will also get the message, I'm sure.

But that still leaves the vast majority of staffing industry owners (and some of their heirs), who I believe will face an increasing challenge to maintain profitability in the years ahead unless they learn better how to gain and hold a "competitive market share," as the authors put it. It is for these many staffing firm operators across the country who may be working harder, but not necessarily smarter, for whom I believe this book can be truly transformational in terms of result.

This volume will also help staffing firm owners of who find themselves working harder just to survive and pay the rent. I hope that they will find the book inspiring enough to revitalize their drive to succeed.

Finkelman and Troper have crafted an easily understood primer that points the way to seven broad areas where staffing firm owners must strive to be excellent. It gives readers scores and scores of staffing industry-specific management practices that will enable them to do so.

Yes, send your staff to as many training sessions as you can, send your kids off to college to get a degree, and make sure that you attend a Staffing Industry Executive Forum at least every other year so you'll know where when and how to sell your business when the time comes (not to mention which software or funding/payrolling package or emerging staffing segment is the best for your particular business and market). But above all else, read these pages carefully to learn how to manage the people side of your people enterprise. Your people will always be the key ingredient to your firm's competitive success.

Peter Yessne
Founder, Staffing Industry Analysts
Founding Publisher, Staffing Industry Report

Acknowledgments

The authors gratefully acknowledge Peter Yessne for suggesting that we write the book and for his support and encouragement in the process; Ron Mester, Barry Asin, Jeff Reeder, and Kay Peterson for their decision to green-light the book and their extraordinary support and encouragement as well as the resources to make this happen; Sharon Thomas, Adriana Kleiman, and Debra Barrath for their superb editing and organizational advice; Robert Wheeler, our designer, for all of his efforts in turning our manuscript into an actual book; and, of course, Staffing Industry Analysts for supplying essential industry data and charts.

Some portions of Chapter 7 first appeared in Staffing Industry Analysts' *SI Review* and *Contingent Workforce Strategies* magazines, or in Staffing Industry Analysts' *Staffing Industry Report* monthly newsletter.

INTRODUCTION

After World War II, U.S. companies so dominated world markets
that they could hire people and promise them a career. Many companies
became complacent. When innovative competitors arose in other countries,
U.S. companies began to lose market share. Hotter competition brought
new products, lower-cost methods of producing old products, quicker
time-to-market, and new competencies to learn. Companies searched
for a way to become more flexible to master the faster pace of change.
Whoever could support the new need for speed and innovation would
quietly become a hero.

Part of the solution was to ramp up with contingent staff when needed.
Companies large and small found that contingent staff enabled them to
take on short-term projects that current employees couldn't handle, bring
in new knowledge they didn't have time to learn, quickly fill difficult jobs,
and accomplish all of this without busting budgets. Staffing firms developed
to service this growing demand. A new industry was born.

From 1970 through 2006, the U. S. staffing industry grew from a daily
workforce of 184,400 to a daily workforce of 2,596,000. That phenomenal
growth comes from producing a product or providing a service that makes
a very big difference for its customers. Staffing firms provide speed, high
quality, and lower costs that a customer could not possibly obtain through
regular, long-term hiring practices.

While corporate hiring could take weeks or months, staffing firms are
able to provide temporary help (contingent workers) within a matter of
days — or even hours. When a critical skill is hard to find, staffing firms
can provide a talented person for a short period. Customers are willing to
pay a premium for such a service whenever not having that skill becomes
expensive. When a company needs a large number of people for a short
period, identifying good candidates may require a huge effort. A staffing

company that already employs many good people can provide them at a fraction of the hiring cost. The most highly competitive staffing firms do a great job of producing at least one of these results for their customers.

Doing these things better than the competition has allowed some staffing firms to grow very fast. As the industry has grown, the most aggressive companies have been able to develop the resources and finesse to buy out select competitors. However, most staffing firms have grown internally by building out their branch networks and expanding their service lines.

Companies fall behind when they don't produce these results very well or don't understand which result matters most to their customers. We will talk later about how to understand customers' needs and match them with staffing service capabilities.

When staffing firms have successfully identified how to compete in their market, how do they make themselves highly competitive? We have found that they excel in seven areas. Each chapter in this book looks at one of the seven attributes that we think distinguish between highly competitive staffing firms and everyone else. Each chapter addresses opportunities and pitfalls in one of the seven areas and answers managers' questions in that area.

1. Great companies excel at **leading people**. The first chapter answers such questions as:

   We have such great people working for us, yet we don't seem to be producing the results we want. How can we produce results through our staffing employees?

   Our company is about to grow to a new level. How do we lead employees through the change needed to grow the company?

   How do you set and communicate performance goals? How often should you review performance and provide feedback? How do you reward your most effective employees — and what do you do with people who don't perform up to par? Is it possible to tame "reckless managers" who make their numbers, but leave a trail of dead bodies behind?

How do you create and support a high-performance environment? How do you create open communication across the branches of a staffing firm so they don't "shoot the messenger"?

2. Great managers excel at **building relationships**. We argue that relationship building drives success in our industry — and nowhere is that more visible than in vendor-on-premises (VOP) programs. How do you use relationships to drive that success? Chapter 2, on Building Relationships, explores such questions as:

How do you build relationships that retain high-quality workers? How do you reduce costs by controlling turnover? How do you recruit and train employees for strong relationship-building skills?

How do you develop strong relationships with customers and with backup suppliers? How do you empower your VOPs for maximum productivity? And how do you manage relationships through crises and change?

3. Highly competitive staffing firms outclass others by **providing services** in a mix that satisfies customers and draws upon their firms' core competence. In the third chapter, Providing Services, we offer some insights into customers' expectations of their staffing suppliers and answer questions like these:

How do you align staffing services with your customers' priorities? How do you execute an effective VOP program? What optional services add profit to a VOP program? What are the essential reporting options that customers expect from a staffing supplier or a VOP?

Which additional human resources services should staffing firms offer to customers? Why is training so important to customers and contingent workers? What training should you provide and when? How can you be sure that your training is effective? How can you provide valid testing services and reduce legal exposure?

How do you structure your staffing firm to provide effective services? How do you avoid attractive, but dysfunctional organizational structures? Why is it essential to separate sales and service? How do you use business reviews to retain customers and improve services?

4. Once they know how to connect their core competence to their customers' needs, highly competitive staffing firms stand out by **marketing and branding** themselves powerfully. Chapter 4 explores answers to questions such as:

   What factors drive staffing firm business strategy? How do you profit from "first mover advantage"? How can a staffing firm use strategic innovations to drive profit even when they are not the first mover?

   How do you compete effectively in a mature service line? How do staffing firms continue to profit from VOP programs as that business model matures?

   How do staffing firms become national or global? How do staffing firms add service lines without jeopardizing the brand? How can a staffing firm cooperate to create a competitive advantage?

5. Forward-thinking and cost-effective staffing firms **exploit technology** in ways that support their business strategy. Technology promises to do everything: increase efficiency, provide cutting-edge services, drive decision-making downward, and even run the whole company! But firms may go beyond the leading-edge to "the bleeding edge" if cutting-edge software crashes computers, misaligns the firm's business processes, or causes staff to struggle with steep learning curves. Chapter 5 asks:

   How can staffing firms profit from the promises of technology and avoid its pitfalls? What other factors should influence technology choices?

   How do vendor management systems change relationships with customers and what should staffing firms do about it?

   How far can staffing firms go with technology-driven business models?

6. All activities involve risk, so top staffing firms protect themselves well by **mitigating risks**. In chapter 6, we examine what risks executives should plan for and how to mitigate them, answering questions like these:

What do you need to know about "co-employment" and why can it jeopardize your company? How can you mitigate the liability? What warning signs of trouble can customers and employees alert you to?

Customers make unrealistic demands. Competitors make offers that customers can't refuse. Sales reps always seem to have an excuse. How do you avoid dysfunctional management responses to these challenges?

How can the "art" of HR management reduce risk for the firm? Many firms use employment tests and performance appraisal systems in ways that would not hold up in court. How does a staffing firm protect itself from this liability?

How do you respond to unreasonable indemnification agreements?

7. When all is said and done, highly competitive staffing firms outshine the rest in **managing profitability**. We address the challenges involved in chapter 7.

Many staffing firms are "driving blind." Without appropriate metrics, it is impossible to profitably guide the firm. What metrics are essential for measuring and driving the bottom line?

Many companies expand with growth for growth's sake and find that their profit doesn't grow along with the firm. Why is "profitable" market share more important than mere growth in the staffing industry? How can companies manage growth profitably?

What do you need to know about factors and funding firms when financing staffing operations and expansion?

Much in the same way that staffing suppliers recommend that their customers outsource non-core processes (i.e., staffing) to them, so, too, staffing firms are well-advised to consider outsourcing their own non-core processes. How far should outsourcing go? And which processes can best be outsourced?

Staffing firms excel when they do these seven things well. Managers in the best staffing firms become good leaders, relationship builders, and contributors to their company's strategy. People who want to become managers in staffing firms need to develop these skills. Companies that want to get into staffing must inventory their capabilities to determine what it will take for them to compete in this growing industry. This book provides insights from experience and research to help staffing industry leaders, professionals, and companies achieve their goals.

We know that we have not answered every question. If reading the book generates more questions for you that might be of interest to managers in the staffing industry, please feel free to contact us.

Jay Finkelman can be reached at jfinkelman@alliant.edu. Jonathan Troper can be reached at jonathan.troper@gmail.com.

Chapter One

LEADING PEOPLE

What does good leadership look like in highly competitive staffing firms? Managers in highly competitive staffing firms lead by providing direction and structure for their employees, contingent workers and customers. They also work collaboratively with other people to produce results. Finally, they create an atmosphere conducive to producing results now and for the future.

Provide Direction and Structure

The best leaders create and communicate a compelling vision of the future, and a vision, mission, values, goals, and action plans that will achieve that vision. A clearly defined and meaningful direction for the company motivates employees and customers and aligns everyone's interests. Excellent leaders understand the world outside their department or company and can explain that world and the best strategy for thriving in it to their troops. We discuss strategy development in chapters 3 and 4.

Create and communicate a compelling vision, mission, values, goals and action plans

When employees and customers know where the company is going and get excited about it, they put out more effort and align their actions in that direction. Achieving this is easier said than done.

Visions, missions, values, goals and action plans must live in employees' and managers' conversations and actions or they disappear from the daily life of the company. Designing a mission statement or values statement and announcing it in a speech or company newsletter is one thing. Ensuring that leaders and opinion makers at all levels of the company integrate the content of those statements into the way they talk and the way they walk is another. Both *talk* and *walk* begin at the top but must involve employees at all levels.

1

At the top, leaders can create excitement about the vision by peppering their speeches with memorable statements and asking their subordinates to do the same. They can translate this excitement into action by leading goal planning and action planning processes where managers and employees determine how to make the mission, vision and values a reality. Finally, leaders can evaluate their progress by listening to employees to find out whether employees got the message and to learn where the vision, goals and action plans need more clarification and fine-tuning.

Although people say that walking the talk is what matters, talking the talk is also critical to helping employees make sense of their organization's direction. Even if managers walk the values of their organization, their subordinates might feel that those values are simply good personal qualities that managers possess. Managers need to let employees know that these attitudes and behaviors are conscious choices that everyone in the organization is expected to make. Without talking about it repeatedly, a mission or values statement can become a dead document that gathers cyberdust on a rarely visited page on the company's intranet. Visions that no one discusses die even more quickly because visions by definition do not exist except in the workers' minds and in their conversations.

Walking the talk does matter, of course. Employees see whether the talk is real based on managers' decisions and actions. Even when a mission, vision or values statement lives on in regular conversations, they become dead to people when managers fail to live by them. Courageous leaders open themselves to being assessed on how well they walk the organization's values and mission and the extent to which their actions achieve the company's goals. When their walk does not match the talk, proactive leaders use executive coaches to help them get back on track.

Consider the following example of a large, privately held staffing company. A talented and creative sales representative attended an early vendor-on-premises (VOP) presentation. During the discussion that followed the formal presentation, the sales representative responded to a particularly vexing question about the ethical issues associated with distributing orders to back-up staffing suppliers. She articulated an operating philosophy of primary supplier conduct that was impressive and persuasive. It was the "right thing" to do. It was also somewhat counter-intuitive in that it entailed giving up some orders that her firm might have been able to fill. But it suggested a brilliant "best practice" that the company ultimately made a hallmark of its approach to enlisting the strongest back-up suppliers in all of its markets. It became part of all subsequent VOP presentations. Equally important, it became part of the company's culture and values.

Compare that example with that of another large staffing firm whose mission, vision and values statements were exceptionally well-crafted and promulgated, but in no way represented the *actual* mission, vision and values that the organization lived by and expected from its managers and employees. Virtually everyone within the organization quickly recognized the inconsistency and the firm's reputation within the staffing industry reflected the reality of its true mission, vision, and values. Employee turnover, especially within management ranks, was indicative of the unfulfilled expectations about the operating philosophy and organizational climate.

What brings a mission, vision, and values statements alive in the first place? Employees must have a reason to own the statements. A sense of ownership can come from participation and inspiration.

Participation can produce ownership, but it isn't always enough. When top management gets employee input while crafting a mission statement, employees are more likely to feel a sense of ownership and understanding. Because they were part of the conversation that developed the mission statement, they know what it means. When top executives airdrop a mission statement onto employees, the employees may regard it as a foreign intrusion into their work. Without the benefit of having heard the conversation that led up to the statement, employees may interpret it very differently from executives who were part of that conversation. Worse, it may seem out of step with their work. However, participation is not enough. A mission statement developed by many people may look like a house with add-on rooms designed in different styles. Chaotic statements die quickly. Whoever leads the development conversation must keep people focused on making the statement clear and compelling.

A great mission, vision, or values statement sounds inspiring. To inspire means to breathe life into something. An inspiring statement energizes people and organizations. What makes a statement inspiring? People feel inspired when they suddenly see a situation in a new way, find a solution to problems that nagged at them, discover a way to make an important goal achievable, or envision a future that they find powerfully meaningful. Great mission statements and action plans give people paths to futures they really want.

Make and communicate decisions effectively

Some decisions just happen. When people are working in their area of expertise, they can often look at a situation, recognize a familiar pattern, and know instantly what decisions they could make and which one will have the best consequences.

But life isn't always that easy. Leaders have to work through other people, so they may not see the day-to-day picture. They have to rely on their people to keep them informed. Leaders hire experts in various areas and have to rely on those experts to apply their specialized knowledge and experience to facilitate strategic decisions and/or implement them. In difficult situations and for non-routine decisions, effective leaders consider several potential solutions before making their decision.

Sometimes, leaders should not make a decision alone; rather, they must design and lead a decision-making process. They need to know when to consider multiple alternatives, when to involve others in the decision-making process, how to communicate those decisions once they are made, and how to ensure adequate implementation. Inadequate involvement and ineffective communication lead to employee resistance or misunderstanding.

Decision-making happens in several stages, which can happen in a sequence or in some cases happen simultaneously.

1. **Identify the decision to make.** Sometimes this step is more difficult than making the actual decision. Leaders must keep their finger on the pulse of the firm. This means monitoring how well the company is doing on every strategic goal and having employees inform them when a critical problem or a great opportunity arises. It also means staying informed about the competitive and regulatory environment and catching any surprises in time to handle them. Leaders rely on

their subordinates to provide critical updates about the company and customers. When leaders possess information, but lack the expertise to assess the implications of that information, they can hire an outside expert to help.

2. **Explore alternative solutions.** Leaders should come up with several possible solutions prior to making a decision, especially when making the wrong decision could be costly. Recent research shows that when people feel that their decision could lead to short-term reward or punishment, their emotions take over. Leaders who go with the first solution they think of may find themselves a victim of old habits or emotion-driven thinking.

   On the other hand, routine decisions that don't challenge a leader's expertise can probably be solved adequately by that first solution. When the cost of making a bad decision is high, there is a personal reward at stake, and/or knowledgeable managers or staff disagree on the best solution, leaders should generate alternative solutions before actually making the decision.

3. **Make the decision.** For complex decisions, leaders should think through the consequences of each potential solution and compare them. Effective leaders consider the effects of the decision at hand on company strategy and on other decisions they are likely to make. For routine decisions, leaders usually know which solution is right without thinking — as long as they have prepared themselves with a search for the right decision to make and good alternative solutions.

4. **Communicate the decision and its rationale.** When the decision is important, unexpected, or negative, leaders must communicate the decision and its rationale to everyone affected by it. Amazingly, managers often fail to complete this important step.

   Tough decisions require excellent communication strategies. People will resist an unpopular decision. Communicating a tough decision requires showing why it had to be made. Management must also show how the results will be beneficial, perhaps even to those who don't like the decision. They must also communicate their commitment to rewarding the people who help implement the decision.

Sometimes, communication is not enough to develop buy-in. In the case of a layoff, the best that leaders can hope for is often grudging acceptance. For tough decisions whose implementation requires a large amount of employee effort, people often are motivated best by participating in the decision-making process.

5. **Work through others to implement the decision.** Leaders usually rely on others to implement the decision. This requires good delegation skills (we discuss producing results through people later in this chapter) and development of buy-in during previous phases of the decision-making process. The principles of managing change (see next section) apply also to implementing decisions.

Leaders must decide how much to involve outside experts or employees in the decision-making process. They often involve others for one of two reasons: when others can provide crucial information or expertise that leaders don't possess or when critical motivation for implementation is enhanced significantly through participation.

Staffing companies face many situations that call for expert help. Those that anticipate a merger or an acquisition, for example, are best served by retaining a consultant in that highly specialized M&A (mergers and acquisitions) arena. Similarly, staffing firms that are considering software upgrades should probably consider retaining the services of someone with that specialized expertise, which tends to be outside the skill sets of the typical staffing manager. In a slightly different vein, staffing suppliers that find themselves faced with significant risk management challenges, such as allegations of sexual harassment or race discrimination, are well-advised to enlist the assistance of external human resources and employment practices experts, typically industrial-organizational psychologists and labor lawyers.

One of the areas staffing managers most frequently solicit expert input is in deciding whether or how to expand (or contract) operations and/ or service lines. Staffing companies prosper or fail based on the wisdom of these decisions. But all too often, staffing managers underestimate the difficulty or misinterpret the apparent "obviousness" of this critically strategic decision. While expanding operations might be an enticing option, for example, a company might be better served by choosing *not* to. Choosing to expand might be neither prudent nor justified, and an outside, impartial consultant can help a company determine if such is the case for it. While it is usually more satisfying to help augment operations, sometimes a consultant can add the most value by discouraging reckless business decisions that might jeopardize the staffing enterprise.

Staffing company leaders also experience several situations where employee involvement helps with decision quality or implementation success. For instance, when businesses face changing situations and frontline workers can provide the eyes and ears that see the changes "up close and personal," managers need to involve them at least in the input phase. Also, when people who will implement or be affected by the decision are likely to resist its implementation, they must be persuaded to accept it. Like most people, executives resist a decision until they have thought it through or have been forced to act by their peers or by the market. Unfortunately, they are often eager to implement the decision without giving subordinates the same time to deal with their emotions and work to overcome their resistance to change.

For example, top management often implements new technologies to work with idealized business processes without regard to the people who will have to run those processes. Many companies spend heavily on technology only to find out that people are resistant, employees don't understand the new plan, or the plan failed to take into account knowledge that frontline workers could have provided.

Sometimes, the decision to undergo a large-scale organizational change that revamps operations calls for employee input at all phases of the decision-making process. Here, leaders have a strategic goal in mind, but admit that they cannot master all the details and understand that employee participation will benefit the quality of the plan. The decision-making process may look more like a learning process in which people contribute what they know to a discussion and everyone learns to view the situation from a new perspective.

Such was the case with a staffing company that was experiencing difficulty with its IT staffing division. Its leadership eventually recognized that they did not really understand how to direct and run an IT operation from its corporate offices. A new senior corporate officer correctly assessed the problem, and transferred operating control to the managers and employees of the IT staffing division. The difference in effective performance was dramatic and almost immediate.

Removed from the corporate systems and operating philosophies that were responsible for the company's success in general office services, the IT staffing division was able to follow the instinct and experience of its own employees. It broke away from the competition with rapid growth and profitability. The participation and empowerment of employees was the most significant factor in making it all happen.

Even when a participatory decision-making process may provide the best result, managers may not use it for various reasons. Welcoming participation may not fit their management style. They may find it hard to let go of control. Often, there simply isn't time for discussions — or so they think.

Style works both ways. Some managers insist on getting input even when it is not needed. Most, however, like to keep control and find it hard to let go. It takes discipline to recognize when a decision should be carried out in a participatory manner and force oneself to let others into the process. It also takes discipline to start the decision-making process in time to allow for participation. Sometimes, there is no time for input because an unexpected situation forced an immediate decision. Often, however, managers don't have time because they failed to plan ahead.

It has become increasingly apparent that the broadest possible input to the decision-making process adds significantly to the quality of those decisions. Consequently, best practices within staffing firms emphasize the openness and "transparency" of the decision-making process. After all, staffing firms are really in the information business — as well as the people business. Anything that impedes the two-way flow of information impedes staffing leaders' ability to make quality decisions as well as their ability to implement them.

Manage change effectively

Several factors influence success and failure in change efforts. The factors are not rocket science, yet most change efforts fail because managers don't ensure that all success factors were in place.

Change comes in two ways: planned or forced. Planned change works well when five factors are in place:

1. **Motivation to change.** People throughout the organization are motivated when they perceive a need for change. Leaders need to plan ways to overcome people's natural resistance to change. Sometimes, all people need is an opportunity to express their fears, be heard, understood, and respected; then they can move on and work toward a vision.

2. **Vision for change.** In order for people to accept that the future will be better for the organization, for their customers, and for themselves, they need to envision how the future will look. A compelling vision makes people feel challenged in a way that calls them to action. That requires giving people time to discuss the details of the vision and to visualize their possible roles in it.

3. **Political support.** The change effort needs support from people with the power to slow down the change or greatly speed it up. People who feel personally supported by their organization are more likely to trust their leaders and support the change effort. If top management required three months to hash out the change program, don't expect staff and customers to need less time, unless staff or customers immediately see the benefits to themselves.

4. **Managing the transition.** Develop action plans and timelines that script the change program. Plan events and discussions designed to gain support from all key stakeholder groups. Plan ways to diagnose how well the change is going. Feedback systems should be sensitive enough to show them the good, the bad, and the ugly. Change leaders need to be brutally honest with themselves about where problems are and what it will take to overcome them.

5. **Sustaining momentum.** After the initial excitement fades, change leaders have to stoke the fires of people's motivation. People need to feel that their efforts are going to lead to results. Celebrating victories along the way helps with that. Human resources systems may need to be modified to reward change and reinforce new behaviors that align with the vision.

If the market forces you to change, try to plan a smooth transition. But if you cannot, there are still several things you can do to manage change more effectively. When the environment tests the company, survival may depend on adaptations that make the company leaner and more results-oriented, yet supportive of the people whose work ensures the company's survival. Companies that use these challenging times to strengthen themselves often find that they are better able to grow when circumstances improve. The best practices for harsh business environments include the following four steps:

1. **Create a sense of urgency, but not a sense of doom.** People will accept changes when they see how harsh the environment really is. Leaders should not hide information from their employees about what is happening in the economy or in the company's niche market. One manager learned that the hard way. At the start of the 1991 recession, despite the fact that the company's clients had obviously been hurting from the effects of a recession for some time, the manager held up a *Wall Street Journal* headline saying "No Recession." Consequently, the manager's staff lost confidence in his ability to assess what was going on in the market. He lost his ability to motivate his staff. As a result, some of the staff lost hope and stopped working hard. Leaders have to walk a fine line between being realistic about the results their employees can produce and letting their employees turn the harsh environment into an excuse for poor performance.

2. **Create an "organizational compass."** An organizational compass differs from a vision. In a harsh environment, leaders may not know what the near future will look like, but they can articulate a general direction that makes sense to their employees and customers. The company culture must align with this general direction so that everyone moves together in the right direction. Leaders who are creating your organizational compass can ask themselves the following questions:

- What promises can you make that delight customers?
- How well does your firm deliver on promises and drive results?
- Are communications and employees' experiences aligned with your firm's strategy and culture?

- Is there effective measurement and feedback of performance and results?
- Is there an effective mechanism for learning and knowledge transfer?
- Are rewards and recognition aligned with intended performance and results?
- Is there a process improvement plan in place?

3. **Provide organizational support.** Leaders provide organizational support in several ways. They regularly demonstrate fairness. They also ensure that supervisors provide employees with the resources and feedback that their direct reports need. Finally, their organizations offer attractive rewards and job conditions. For more information on this, refer to the section titled "Create a Productive Atmosphere" later in this chapter.

4. **Take advantage of opportunities.** Even a harsh business environment provides opportunities. For instance, in a slow market, good employees are easier to find. Top management can hold their human resources department accountable for hiring higher-caliber employees.

Become lean and nimble

Some of the most difficult but rewarding changes come from restructuring. Leaders make their companies competitive by structuring the company so that it can carry out strategy decisively and flexibly — the way an efficient predator is designed to run down its prey. Efficient predators are smarter and/or faster than their prey and more nimble than their competitors. They focus their energy on the best food sources, and they don't waste it. When they live in a changing environment, they learn to change with it.

Smart firms today must be nimble, and nimble firms tend to have a flatter organizational structure. Hierarchies are inefficient and slow. They are also costly and not particularly productive. Multiple levels of management rarely pay for themselves. Ask yourself whether you really need branch managers and sales managers and operations managers and area managers and district managers and regional managers — all in a redundant hierarchy. Probably not.

Flatter structures enable leaders to delegate decisions to people on the front lines. Decisions need to be made as close to the customer and the action as possible. In fast-paced staffing environments, decisions should be made by employees out in the field. It is often management arrogance, and perhaps management defensiveness, that insists on centralizing decision-making that really belongs in the field. Trust your field operation, or acknowledge that you have the wrong field operation in place and change it.

Smart firms are "lean and mean." Lean and mean is more than a catchphrase, it is a philosophy of doing business in challenging economic environments. It saves you money, but it has other advantages as well. It enables you to reward your best performers more effectively. It creates an exciting and demanding work environment that appeals to your best performers and discourages those who may have elected to "retire" on the job. It is an automatic form of job enrichment that encourages your aspiring staff to stretch to get the job done.

Leaders of nimble organizations share information freely. That's because information is the lifeblood of the business. The greatest risk involved in information sharing is not losing control of proprietary or confidential information; it is keeping sufficient information from staff who need it. Those who might be inclined to misuse the information have other ways to get it. Limiting information flow tends to emasculate management and render staff impotent and resentful. Rumors quickly fill in for credible information — and they tend not to be flattering.

When leaders empower their frontline managers with information and decision-making power, the firm serves customers better and is better-positioned to take advantage of opportunities. Frontline staffing managers are typically closest to their customers, although smart senior staffing management is learning the utility of staying as close as possible to their (larger) customers as well. Information is power in the staffing industry and frontline managers usually control the information and "intelligence." Staffing companies that have shifted decision-making and operating control to frontline managers tend to be more competitive.

The most nimble and effective companies have learned to move decision-making to where the information first flows from their customers.

While this may not come naturally to many staffing company founders and entrepreneurs who have become competitive by "selling" their own drive, initiative and market savvy to their employees and customers, the superior track record of those who have forced themselves to do this is compelling.

Many opportunities require upper management support. In order to hear about those opportunities, top management must listen to what frontline managers have to say. Flat organizations require efficient and sometimes creative systems of two-way communication among managers at all levels.

Be consistent and courageous

It isn't easy to implement the ideas presented so far. They require consistency and courage.

When business environments change dramatically over short periods, leaders can't always know what tack to take next. Yet, employees need consistency from their leaders. Consistent management is always important, but it is especially important in adverse business climates. In a national study of 1,000 U.S. employees, Maritz Inc. found that when employees perceive their firms' senior management as acting consistently, they reported significantly higher job satisfaction, employee recommendation of company products and services, teamwork and tenure at their companies. Effective leaders decide which things to be consistent about and which to change as the business climate alters, and they communicate these decisions to their people.

Good leaders face the facts of the market and use those facts to make difficult decisions. Then, they communicate those decisions openly. For instance, a national firm may depend on aggressive pricing to keep its large customers. But price wars result in everyone being unprofitable. A courageous leader may decide that using price cuts to keep large, but barely profitable accounts just doesn't make sense. Instead, the firm can be internally honest about the true costs associated with each account and use opportunistic strategies to develop business relationships with large customers that *are* profitable. Those strategies are discussed in detail in chapters 3 and 4.

Produce Results through People

Effective leaders manage talent and performance. They care about their people and the results that their people produce. They select and retain the best talent both during times of growth and downsizing. They learn what attracts the best people and what keeps them there. They recognize potential and develop it. They also inspire their people to produce the best results. When their people perform, they reward their performance creatively.

Talent management

Selecting and retaining the best people isn't just a task for the best times. When the economy hits a rough patch and your company downsizes, you can bet good money that other companies are downsizing, too. That puts good people on the street. That's the time to lure the best talent into the company. Effective leaders learn what attracts the best people and what keeps them there. That makes it possible to hire during lean times and to keep top talent when the economy is so good that recruiters come calling to steal your best.

Effective leaders recognize potential and develop it. They hire people with skills that align with the company's competitive advantage. They write succession plans to identify the next generation of leaders. Then, they provide training to develop employees' knowledge, skills and attitudes and special assignments to high-potential employees to broaden their horizons and develop their expertise.

Smart staffing managers always select the strongest possible direct reports, while weak and defensive managers naively select non-threatening subordinates who usually turn out to be less effective. This, of course, is totally counterproductive. There is little question but that in the staffing industry, firms are overwhelming dependent upon their internal staff in order to properly serve their customers and remain competitive. There is no higher priority in staffing firms than to recruit, select and retain the best possible internal staff. We discuss some best practices in testing and evaluation in subsequent chapters.

Succession plans list the high-level positions in the company and employees who could be developed over the coming months or years to fill them. Promotable employees will feel motivated by hearing that top management views them as a significant asset to the organization and is likely to promote them if they excel and opportunities open up. The human resources department can team up with top management to identify the skills that promotable employees will need to excel in the jobs to which they are likely to be promoted and then design training and stretch assignments that will develop those skills.

Training more than pays for itself when it is targeted to developing skills that enhance employees' effectiveness. It is the sure sign of an excellent company that values its employees and their skills. Investing in your staff is especially crucial as you ask fewer employees to do more work. They will notice, appreciate it and reciprocate. Training also reduces unwanted turnover, because good employees value companies that enable them to keep learning and keep their skills fresh. You need to do it.

Employees need training from the first moment they arrive. *New hire orientations* (NHO) boost productivity by setting expectations and decreasing the number of times that new employees have to take experienced employees' time with commonly asked questions. Some of the content of an NHO can be turned into a pre-employment peek into the job. Research shows consistently that new hires who saw a *realistic job preview* prior to accepting the job become productive more quickly and last longer than new hires who did not.

Every company does things a little differently. *Job skills training* provides employees with a picture of how their job is done. It may be supplemented with *computer skills training* to show them when and how to use the company's software.

The most effective employees keep improving soft skills that give the company its strategic advantage, such as relationship-building skills and communication skills. *Soft skills training* may sound like an extra until a competitor with more sophisticated employees steals a valued client.

No company can grow without *leadership development*. Effective leaders lead best when they have effective leaders following them! This begins with supervisory training for anyone promoted to a supervisory position. Employees who excel at their work but haven't supervised people before don't know how to set goals, help others to set goals, delegate specific projects, or manage others' performance. As they rise in the organization, people need to develop management and leadership skills, including performance management, talent management, vision-building, and action planning. Developing these skills not only requires formal training but also informal mentoring and formal coaching, developmental 360-degree feedback, and stretch assignments.

Developmental 360-degree feedback is an assessment technique that requires a manager's supervisors, peers, and subordinates to rate him/her on how well they lead. Then, a coach delivers the feedback to the manager and designs assignments that will help the manager grow skills in areas where he/she is weak and build on his/her strengths.

High-potential leaders should be given stretch assignments — tasks designed to make them develop strengths that they will need when they get promoted — and mentoring. Mentoring only works when an experienced leader cares deeply about his/her protégé's success and can translate complex wisdom into actionable suggestions that an up-and-coming manager can try out. No experienced leader should be assigned to mentor someone they wouldn't go out of their way to defend in a tough spot. No experienced leader should be assigned to mentor *anyone* if the leader is not excellent as a role model and a trainer.

In our experience, best internal training practices within the staffing industry incorporate the following elements:

- Maximum use of self instruction and computer assisted training techniques when employees are distributed geographically or not available at the same time;
- Maximum use of active and interactive training techniques when employees can meet together;
- Maximum involvement of management (corporate and local) in the training process, including involvement in determining learning objectives, communicating the importance of training to employees prior to and after training, and following up to support trainees in implementing new skills on the job;
- Maximum incorporation of learning and job performance metrics in order to assess and improve the efficacy of the training process — as well as individual mastery; and

- Maximum use of "refresher"-type training to insure retention, expand learning opportunities and update training content.

Training costs money. In order to ensure that the firm uses this money wisely, leaders should ask human resources planners to do two things. First, they should design training based on needs assessments. A good needs assessment begins with a business case — a cost-benefit analysis that identifies the desired results and scrutinizes the cost of providing those results. Then, it analyzes the organization, the task, and the target audience and communicates those findings to instructional designers who produce a training solution that fits the situation. It also provides an evaluation plan to determine how well the training program delivered the desired results and explains why. This produces lessons learned for use in the next training design cycle. Sometimes, a needs assessment saves money by identifying solutions other than training that are more effective in producing the desired results.

Second, they should ensure that the firm doesn't lose people after it spends the money on training them. This can be done by making the firm a great place to work. Attractive career paths, an atmosphere that is great to work in, competitive pay, and supportive managers all make it hard to leave an organization.

Effective talent management gets the right people in the door, prepares them for their work, and keeps them committed to the company. But that's only the first part of an effective staffing firm's strategy for producing great results through people. The rest of the strategy involves methods for improving people's performance.

Performance management

The best leaders inspire their people to produce the best results. They set goals and reward results creatively. Rewards come in many kinds of packages, some of which don't cost the company as much as salary increases do. They also deliver negative consequences for bad behavior and poor results. While they give people a chance, leaders provide consequences and then let go of people who cannot or will not produce. They take action quickly to stop inappropriate behavior, especially when that behavior damages other employees' motivation.

Recognition and reward for producing excellent results decrease turnover and shine a light on individuals so they become role models for others. While providing recognition and reward for excellent performers may seem like an obviously important step to take, identifying the best performers may not be so obvious. In better economic times, the best performers are regarded as superstars whose individual achievements (typically in sales) set them apart from their colleagues. The problem is that so-called superstars may undermine total team performance and create unhealthy staff resentment. It is important that you carefully manage your superstars and reinforce your true team players.

Select metrics, set goals and communicate performance

Let performance metrics guide your operations and decisions. The best firms utilize a variety of metrics that serve as key measures of their effectiveness with respect to customers, staff and financial performance. Lesser firms do not believe in or trust performance metrics and do not use them to manage their business. Make sure that you measure the right things. Sometimes, leaders focus on what is easiest to measure instead of focusing on measuring behaviors and results that enact the company strategy.

SMART Goals Provide Paths to Achievement

Research has demonstrated for decades the power of goal-setting and feedback, and the importance of doing it right.

SMART goals are Specific, Measurable, Achievable yet challenging, Relevant to the person and the organization, and Trackable.

Specificity and measurability ensure that everyone can tell the extent to which a goal is being achieved. People need feedback in order to know whether they are going in the right direction or putting out enough effort. Vague goals make feedback difficult to interpret.

The best staffing firms incorporate precise "activity"-type measures, in addition to the more traditional performance measures, such as the number of telemarketing calls initiated, completed, reaching viable decision-makers, and finally, the number of telemarketing calls that actually result in new business — or significant incremental business. Excellent software is available to facilitate this process.

The most exciting goals feel like a challenge. People get bored or slack off when goals are too easy. However, too much challenge provokes people to give up. While minimum standards must be the same for everyone, each person differs in his or her sense of their capability; so great leaders set goals for each subordinate in his or her sweet spot.

Relevant goals are aligned with organization strategy and feel personally meaningful to the people trying to achieve them. A salesperson who lives to win will find it very motivating to set goals focused on stealing market share from competitors. A VOP manager who loves taking care of people will feel proud about reducing staff turnover and will work hard to achieve that.

Trackable goals have a "by when" attached. Progress reports track milestones toward goal achievement so everyone knows where they stand. Make sure that all parties who can influence a goal's achievement receive this information and pay attention to it.

Shared bonuses are an obvious way to reward team players — and their staffing teams. A good option is a hybrid approach that incorporates both group and individual incentives, which tends to optimize team behavior, insure team support of the superstars, and still provide individual achievement incentives. Moving the most effective team players into leadership and ultimately management positions is another effective technique to reward your best team players publicly.

After leaders select metrics, they must determine what standards to reward and what minimum standards workers must maintain in order for to keep their jobs. Effective leaders communicate those standards in a variety of ways. They can embed messages that describe standards in emails, employee newsletter columns, and presentations. Most important, they can hold one-on-one goal-setting conversations with subordinates and ensure that all managers do the same. Subordinates should leave these conversations with SMART goals and a commitment to exceeding the standards. Managers should leave knowing what extra support — such as training and feedback — they need to provide to subordinates to bolster their subordinates' skills and motivation.

These kinds of conversations don't just happen at goal-setting discussions and performance appraisals. They also happen when managers delegate specific projects. Good leaders delegate effectively.

How to Delegate Effectively

Effective leaders regularly delegate projects and ongoing responsibilities so they can focus their own time on supervising and planning for the future. They select trustworthy subordinates with the right skills and attitudes. Then, they set their subordinates up for success by taking these steps:

- **Select tasks to be delegated.** Effective leaders delegate tasks that they don't have time for, that could be better handled by someone with special skills, and that cost less when others handle them. Leaders surround themselves with excellent people. Those people have expertise that complements the leader's skills. Effective leaders delegate tasks that call on that expertise to the people around them.

- **Turn tasks to be delegated into projects.** Projects end with results and begin with a timelined action plan. It's more satisfying for a subordinate to work on something with a visible product that gives them a sense of pride. An action plan tells who will do what by when and what the expected result will be. Whether the leader or the subordinate writes the action plan, everyone who reads it sees clearly what needs to be done.

- **Choose your delegate wisely.** The chosen delegate must have the knowledge, skills and attitudes to handle the task. If you are developing an employee by giving her a stretch assignment, make sure to select a mentor who can support that person.

- **Communicate expectations clearly.** Discuss the project with the delegate and make sure that she understands what needs to be done and commits to producing the results. First, leaders explain why this project is important and discuss the action plan (who will do what and by when) and the resources needed to make it happen. Then, they agree on how and when the subordinate will report back on progress and what kinds of obstacles or problems warrant communication with the leader. Then, they ask what support the subordinate will need in order to complete the project. Finally, the leader commits to providing support but getting out of the subordinate's way and the subordinate commits to producing the results and reporting on progress.

- **Make sure to follow up.** If the subordinate doesn't take the initiative to report progress and raise red flags when there is a problem, the leader contacts the subordinate to ask for an update. Effective leaders give the support that their people need, but don't micromanage.

- **Expect results and celebrate success.** Effective leaders expect the project to be completed. If the subordinate turns in partial work, the leader asks for completion. When the subordinate finishes the project, effective leaders give credit where credit is due. Public recognition of significant results boosts strong subordinates' pride and provides a role model for others to follow. Holding an after-action review where the subordinate and leader give each other feedback on how the process went helps improve delegation the next time around.

Communicate performance regularly and consistently

Strong managers communicate performance results to their employees and let them know regularly how they are doing. When leaders set clear metrics that make sense for each job, managers find it much easier to communicate how well each employee is doing. They communicate excellent performance in public and privately, and discuss nonperformance privately, but involve the human resources department in issuing warnings. The most common performance communication tool is the performance appraisal (or performance review). Performance appraisals are as common as job interviews and coffee breaks — but they may do more harm than good unless you are careful and consistent in their implementation.

Historically, top management has seen performance reviews as a tool to boost productivity, while frontline managers have used performance reviews to maintain employee morale through "grade inflation." It is simply less stressful for managers to "be nice" and convey positive evaluations rather than more candid, negative evaluations. Perhaps surprisingly, though, this phenomenon occurs even when salary increases are tied to performance reviews, for much the same reason; the only difference is that the scale of salary-increase-to-performance-rating shifts down to accommodate the inflated evaluation.

This is an improper use of a valuable human resource management tool, for a variety of reasons:

- The performance appraisals do not accurately reflect employees' true performance.
- Management loses the opportunity for honest evaluation and discussion of the employees' performance and opportunities for improvement.
- Employees develop unrealistic and unreasonable expectations for compensation and promotion.

Some readers will be surprised to learn that the courts consider performance appraisals a form of "testing." Certain selection procedures, such as job interviews, are legally classified as traditional testing instruments, though most managers don't realize that they must treat them with the caution due such instruments. Performance appraisals fall in a similar category, even if the managers don't consistently utilize them in that fashion. As such, they technically require validation, particularly when managers use them in a manner that may adversely affect an employee's job status or conditions of employment. This is something you may wish to review with an industrial-organizational psychologist or an employment lawyer. Validation essentially asks whether a testing device does what it purports to do. We discuss such issues further in chapter 6, "Mitigating Risk."

Reward good results

Effective leaders reward good results. But rewards are not a one-size-fits-all proposition.

What counts as a reward? Do the "rewards" currently being doled out actually motivate the employees? Everyone likes recognition, bonuses, and pay increases. However, what makes the biggest difference depends on the person. Some people care most about having a supportive boss or moving ahead in their career. For someone itching for a change, a special assignment that gives them a taste of a new career direction will feel like a reward. For someone with a clear idea in mind, a move toward their desired position will be rewarding. A new mother or father may desire a shift to more flexible hours or comp time. A bonus may matter most to someone who just purchased a home. To succeed in any of these scenarios, good leaders must get to know what their subordinates want.

Even little rewards matter. Perks like bottled water (no matter how silly and unnecessary you may think it is), good coffee, occasional pastries and free lunches make people feel supported. They mean more than you might imagine to most employees, regardless of their level and compensation. The perks — or lack thereof — deliver a strong message about how you regard your staff. It is an emotional reaction, so don't try to analyze it rationally. But as you are expecting your staff to do more, it would be especially unfortunate to engage in petty economies that will inevitably be misconstrued — and backfire.

Senior management cannot be expected to learn all of their workers' aspirations and levels of motivation and job satisfaction. They should delegate this to line managers while providing line managers a role model. The best times to learn about individual aspirations are over lunch or any other informal conversation or during one-on-one goal-setting discussions and performance reviews.

When the company does well due to teamwork, shared bonuses send a message that teamwork made a difference. On the other hand, across-the-board salary increases not tied to performance improvements send the wrong message.

Assess penalties for poor results

Effective leaders also deliver negative consequences for poor results and bad behavior. While they give people a chance, effective leaders provide consequences and then let go of people who cannot or will not produce.

Signs that Staffing Management is Failing

- **Isolation** from customers and prospects — and in the most egregious instances, from internal staff. This is somewhat of a pathological sign that a failing manager is withdrawing from the unpleasant realities of a working environment that they cannot master or control.
- **Preoccupation** with the administrative aspects of supervision and management — to the detriment of the inspirational, coaching and leadership elements. Administrative work always expands to fit the time allotted. Effective managers allocate as little time as possible. Failing managers allocate most of their business day.
- **Rationalization** that everybody is in the same boat — and that there is nothing that can be done about difficult business conditions anyway. In reality, unless a firm enjoys a truly dominant market share, there is always something that can be done — probably at the expense of competitors!
- **Blaming** someone else who may be a convenient scapegoat at the time and probably not in a position to defend themselves effectively. It is a classic symptom of poor management that they seek scapegoats to deflect criticism from themselves. (That also buys time to hire or promote and develop the next scapegoat!)
- **Justification** for failure with excuses that may be legitimate on their face — but should have been anticipated and/or discounted long ago. Using workers' comp issues to explain poor performance in California is an obvious example.

Managers need to communicate performance to employees prior to taking action. When employee behavior is particularly bad, managers should issue warnings right away and document those warnings, keeping the human resources department updated on any warnings issued. Good managers consult their human resources department to ensure that they follow consistent, legally defensible procedures to issue warnings and terminate poor performers.

No one really enjoys terminating poor performers — nor should they. And sometimes an adverse business environment is used as the disingenuous excuse to invite non-performers to leave: "We would love to retain your services, but we just don't have enough business to justify it. Thank you for your service to this firm." An improving business climate, on the other hand, makes it easier to rationalize the retention of marginal performers. Staffing firms are simply more capable of carrying such employees during good times. But that is not what an effective organization should do with its human resources.

When poor performance first crops up, managers should analyze its causes to see the extent to which it results from factors that can be changed. To the extent that the cause is in business processes or something else that managers can control, leaders should take action to address those causes. Even when poor performance stems from the performer, it is often possible to turn it around when it stems from a gap in the person's knowledge, skills, or attitudes and when the person is open to change. Training, coaching, mentoring, outside reading and other methods can build a worker's knowledge and skills. Good leaders can often inspire poor performers to turn their attitudes around.

If these tactics don't work, managers must recognize when it is time to give up and terminate the poor performer. How much effort to spend on turning around a poor performer is a judgment call. Human resources consultants can help determine what it will take to get at the causes of a worker or manager's poor performance.

Tame reckless managers

Some managers merely perform below standards. Others are outright reckless. Effective leaders take action quickly to stop inappropriate behavior, especially when that behavior damages other employees' motivation. Otherwise, that behavior can become a cancer that eats at a department or even the whole organization.

We have all known reckless managers. Often they mean well; sometimes they do not. Either way, they pose a serious risk to their company if leaders do not exert control over their conduct and activities. It is too easy to ignore their behavior as immature and brush aside their comments as not serious. But their colleagues, subordinates — and the courts — may not view it that way.

How to Respond to a Failing Manager

- **Coaching.** Even senior management can benefit from performance feedback and direction. Absent feedback, the manager may not even know that he is failing — or what to do in response. (Of course, with really senior management, there may not be anyone available — or qualified or gutsy enough — to coach or to mentor them! In this situation, it may be best to call in an outside executive coach.)
- **Repositioning.** Sometimes a manager with potential has simply been incorrectly assigned to a position that is not best suited to their skill sets and inclination. This can happen at any level of management. Sometimes the "Peter Principle" may be operating — in which a manager has been promoted beyond her level of competence. (For example, not every great sales representative has the skills to be a manager.)
- **Demotion.** Sometimes repositioning may require a downgrade to allow a manager to operate within his competence and confidence level. It is best to be certain that this is not a response to the shortcomings and failures of more senior management first, however. (Be aware that this is a drastic step that typically engenders significant defensiveness and resentment — and often does not work as a consequence.)
- **Hiring or promoting above.** Sometimes it becomes necessary to hire new talent above the failing manager, in order to respond to deficiencies without appearing to denigrate the deficient manager. Regrettably, this tactic is rarely more effective or more face-saving than "demotion" because of its obvious transparency.
- **Termination.** Sometimes terminating the failing manager is best for all parties — and coaching or repositioning has not worked. As before, it is essential to insure that the terminated individual is not being used as a scapegoat for a more senior manager who should have been removed from their own position instead.

Most companies understand that they bear some level of responsibility for the conduct of their managers and supervisors. Depending on the circumstances, adequacy of responses and jurisdictions, this may range from "strict liability" to no liability. Only employment lawyers can make this call.

It's amazing but true that these people are often regarded and treated as "the life of the party." Alternatively, they may be respected for their "candor and directness" — managers who can be relied upon to say what they think. Unfortunately, this level of candor and lack of "political correctness" is a double-edged sword. No one, especially not the reckless manager, can correctly anticipate how individuals will react to others' language, gestures and contact.

How to Prevent and Tame Reckless Management

First, sensitize everyone to the difference between appropriate and inappropriate behavior. This sensitization can be accomplished in a variety of ways:

- Set a good example. Nothing undermines desired management behavior as much as when senior management violates it, even in jest.
- Establish and publish guidelines. Don't make anyone guess (or assume) how they are expected to behave. They may guess wrong!
- Provide training regarding appropriate behavior. All staff must be trained so that they know what their responsibilities are and what is considered appropriate behavior. Don't assume that good behavior is obvious. It isn't. Encourage everyone to confront and report violations.
- Reinforce the training. Don't assume that you can train once and forget about it. That may be adequate, but it may not be.
- Document the training and the participants. This obvious step can prevent your having to scramble to respond to future claims that your company was negligent by not providing adequate training.
- Employ a "multi-modality" approach to sensitization. Employ training programs (Web-based, CD-ROM, videotapes, or standup

trainers), written anti-harassment and anti-discrimination guidelines, management reinforcement and appropriate discipline to support the message.

- Utilize MBWA (management by walking around). Do this frequently and randomly. Never permit managers or supervisors to control access to their people. Doing so could inadvertently encourage misbehavior.
- Practice a true open-door policy. This has tremendous utility in shaping good management behavior — and constraining reckless behavior — if practiced judiciously.
- Investigate alleged infractions. A professionally conducted investigation continues to be among the best defenses against sex and race discrimination and harassment claims.
- Act immediately. It is vital that you confront violators immediately and take appropriate action. Never permit actual misconduct to go unchallenged. Doing so sends an inappropriate message to all involved.
- Protect employees against retaliation. It is your obligation to do whatever is reasonable to protect accusers and witnesses from the possibility of retaliation. The consequences of not guarding against foreseeable and demonstrated retaliation may be more serious than for the initial alleged harassment.

For example, a regional manager could not control her need to engage in sexual banter with men and woman under her supervision — and many were offended by it. Despite a number of warnings, the behavior did not stop. Instead, vulgarity crept into most of her staff meetings and one-on-one conversations. She eventually resigned when confronted with the almost universal discomfort with her ongoing lack of professionalism and impending disciplinary action. She also believed that her conduct was innocuous. She just did not get it.

Many leaders have had to fire managers or employees who appeared not to have a clue about the way their actions were perceived by subordinates or peers. This is never pleasant, especially when it might have been avoided. While there are no absolute guidelines, it is good practice to err on the side of caution. These managers need to be exposed to the potential consequences of their behavior, which they regard as "innocent."

Reckless managers tend to focus on themselves, not on how their behavior affects others. That is why they need coaching, mentoring, and perhaps discipline. They may have the leadership qualities needed to be effective, but they often come with considerable baggage. Of course, the baggage must be dealt with in a manner that does not intrude on their rights and privacy. That is the art of management.

Consider "360-degree" performance appraisals

Industrial-organizational psychologists have been incorporating employee and peer ratings of their managers into corporate performance management and evaluation programs for more than a decade. These "360 degree" appraisals are becoming increasing popular because employees and peers can see important elements of management skill and competence can easily elude the scrutiny of "superiors" in an organizational setting.

In such a performance appraisal, human resources or industrial-organizational psychologists give a validated survey to each manager and that manager's subordinates, peers, and superiors. The survey measures well-recognized managerial skills and can be edited to focus on skills that align with company strategy. Senior managers can use the results for salary and promotion decisions or for development purposes (as a needs assessment for training, coaching, or stretch assignments). The same survey should not be used for both salary/promotion and for development because survey takers tend to respond a bit differently depending on the purpose.

In the past, unenlightened managers (and even ordinary employees) thought that only the opinion of their bosses mattered. Their efforts were devoted to impressing — and perhaps fooling — those above them in the organizational hierarchy with the perceived power to determine their salaries, promotions and careers. While that, unfortunately, is still the norm in most staffing companies today, progressive companies are incorporating elements of 360-degree feedback in their performance appraisal systems. And they are increasingly the companies that are most competitive in the marketplace as well!

Effective talent management and performance management strategies bring in the best people and get the best from them. This works well at the individual level. But the strongest leaders also lead well through their effect on the whole organization.

Create a Productive Atmosphere

Effective leaders create an atmosphere conducive to producing results. First, their own actions provide a role model for others in their organization. They lead with integrity and professionalism. Second, they ensure that the organization sets people up for success by providing the resources, rewards, fairness, and other support that their workers need. Third, they create an atmosphere of open communication and manage conflicts constructively. Finally, they value their people's contributions and value diversity.

Lead by example with integrity and professionalism

Employees and customers can count on leaders who are known for integrity and accountability, diplomacy and fairness. Integrity and accountability comes from alignment between the leader, his/her role, the goals they seek to achieve, the rules of fair play, and the support that his/her followers need from the leader in order to succeed. Effective leaders promote integrity with their words and their example. When leaders fall short in professionalism or integrity, the organization eventually suffers.

Great leaders make promises and follow through on them. Their actions are those that people would expect from someone trying to fulfill the promise. Or, if the leader was particularly creative, people can see in retrospect that the leader's actions were consonant with achieving the goal.

Rather than playing it safe, great leaders take the risk of making big promises. The bigger the promise a leader can fulfill, the greater his/her integrity. They may start with smaller promises and build up to something big, but eventually, they learn to play in the big leagues.

This doesn't mean that they flout standards of conduct in order to achieve their goals. Look at societies where bribes and graft are common to see what happens when cutting corners becomes part of people's daily expectation; their economies are held back by the waste of corruption. Effective leaders enforce ethical rules of conduct in their organizations and in their industry. Corporate scandals in the early 2000s underlined the cost of dramatic lapses in integrity. But an organization can experience death by a thousand cuts when little white lies proliferate.

Consider the case of a staffing entrepreneur who was a pioneer in establishing VOP programs throughout California. The company gained a major client by promising that it would be able to staff specific, complex and difficult-to-fill IT positions at a very competitive bill rate — along with an array of other service lines that were more in the mainstream of its recruiting capabilities. It turned out that there was a reason why the company's competitors were having difficulty filling those IT positions — and why they were charging the premium rates that motivated the customer to entertain bids from other suppliers.

When it became apparent that the company had dramatically overstated its IT recruiting capabilities, it had to take immediate action to avoid disappointing the customer. First, it acknowledged that it had inadvertently misrepresented its ability to recruit the required IT workers. Then the company subcontracted two of its competitors that were able to fill those positions consistently, paying to them their full billing rate, yet charging back to its customer at its originally agreed-upon billing rate. Despite the fact that the company was paying considerably more than it was charging, it never attempted to hire those workers away from its competitors in order to avoid paying the competitors' mark-up.

The company lost money, overall, for more than a year with this customer, until it voluntarily offered to increase the billing rate in the second year of the agreement. But the best part was the reputation that the staffing entrepreneur gained for honoring its commitments, even when they were made naively and unrealistically. The customer was impressed, as were its competitors. The company retained that customer for over a decade, and the best competitors were always willing to serve as its back-up suppliers. The customer also served as an enthusiastic and willing reference for its VOP programs, which facilitated the acquisition of a number of new customers. Clearly, the staffing company made a good investment with its ethical behavior.

When great leaders fail to accomplish what they promised, they admit it and set goals for themselves that they can achieve. Good leaders speak honestly about what gets in the way of achieving goals, but they play the blame game sparingly. When others' efforts help fulfill the promises, great leaders give those people credit.

Followers want to put out such effort when they see their leaders as role models. A manager was hired to start an accounting and financial services division for one of the largest regional full-service staffing company. He quickly drew notice for the difference in the way he operated his division — and a concomitant difference in how rapidly it became profitable. Fifteen years later, the manager's branch was the second-best performer nationally among hundreds of branches for a very demanding international financial staffing company.

His managers asked what they could learn from his success so they could share his best practices. His answer was simply that they should hire managers who were willing to sell — and not simply willing to manage. "I lead by example" were his exact words. Obvious? Of course. But so few managers of multi-million dollar operations actually do it. Somehow, branch and even sales managers inexorably come to believe that they are above direct selling. And that is how they begin to fail. Sales managers accrue many benefits by including sales in their management role, but how to make that inclusion is an art.

While fulfilling on the promises that they make, effective leaders also pay attention to the other people around them. They may be brutally honest, but they use diplomacy. That means speaking difficult truths in a language that people will listen to. It means timing their messages for the audience. The best time is as soon as possible so that the listener is not preoccupied when he/she hears the message and has enough time left to do something about it.

When effective leaders make decisions that affect people negatively or differentially, they consider how to make the decisions fairly so that negative impacts hit where they should and people are rewarded differently only for good reasons. They also communicate their decisions in ways that make workers see the fairness of their decision-making processes.

Sales managers should lead by example

Why should sales managers lead by example?

- Leading by example facilitates "multi-level" selling to a customer. This typically entails sales managers calling upon a higher level of decision-maker than the sales representatives who report to them, and senior staffing management calling upon the executive officers of the customers or prospects.
- Leading by example with customers provides both a level of protection in the event that an account manager goes to the competition.
- A selling manager also has a greater opportunity to position your firm for a greater "share of wallet" within existing customers.
- A manager can be a far more effective ally in developing a "closing" strategy if the manager has actually called on the prospect *independent* of the sales representative.
- A manager may be able to access decision-makers above the level of the initial screeners whom the sales representative typically encounters — who may only have the power to say "no."

Of course, being a doer too much of the time can derail managers who don't spend enough of their time supervising, planning or coordinating across departments. Hence, sales managers should limit the amount of time they devote to selling and consider which of three approaches they should take:

1. Consistently be in the field with sales representatives — making team sales calls to both prospects and customers.
2. Consistently be in the field with sales representatives — making team sales calls to prospects only.
3. Consistently be in the field, but mostly alone — making individual sales calls to their own prospects or to the prospects of their sales representatives (and with the "permission" of their sales representatives).

Each approach has its unique advantages and limitations:

1. Team sales calls to both prospects and customers is very supportive of the sales representative but may not always be the most efficient use of a manager's time — largely depending upon how many reps are being managed.

2. Team sales calls to prospects only is a more efficient business *development* vehicle but a less effective business *retention* vehicle.

3. Sole sales calls by managers may make the best use of a manager's personal sales ability — and may appear very time-efficient — but risks putting the manager into competition with the sales representatives and also deprives the representatives of the benefit of mentoring and team strategy. Thus it may serve to make the sales representative less effective and efficient in the field. After all, the point of sales management is to *manage* other people — not simply direct sales.

Best of "Best Practices". The overall best practice is probably a manager who maintains a limited number of individual prospects, spends the bulk of time *in the field* developing and supervising the sales representatives for which the manager has responsibility and visits all customers with a frequency determined by customer size and potential vulnerability. Of course, the parameters of each of these activities need to be adjusted as a function of many factors, including the number and experience level of the sales reps for whom the manager is responsible and the competitive environment in which they operate.

Thus, while there is no generic absolute best practice, a good bet appears to be a balance of targeted individual selling, significant facilitation of the sales activities of the reps, and a level of visibility with all key customers that insures retention regardless of the rep. The most critical best practice is the ability and willingness of managers to spend the bulk of their days *in the field* — especially during the prime selling hours of the day. That requires that they deal with routine administrative duties either before or after prime selling time — such as meetings, reports, preparation of presentations and performance reviews.

It also requires that managers be willing to delegate certain responsibilities to qualified subordinates. And most important, it requires that they trust their inside staff to do *their* job — and that they leave them alone to do it — after insuring that they have the proper tools. In the case of one successful manager, his inside staff is conditioned to tell *him* when to get out of the office in the morning to sell — but also to ask for assistance if *they* feel that they need it. Of course he also reviews computerized key metrics on a daily basis each evening — not leaving very much to chance.

Worst Practices. In today's competitive environment, with continued pressure on margins and an ongoing emphasis on cost containment — and preferably reduction — traditional management approaches within the staffing industry staffing are failing, as are traditional managers. It is no longer sufficient — nor credible to internal staff — to manage from within private offices. There is no acceptable rationale for not being with customers and for not calling on prospects. There are plenty of excuses, however. And the *legitimate* excuses should be attended to before and after selling hours.

Provide organizational support

Acting with integrity and leading by example are important acts of leadership, but they are not enough to create a productive atmosphere. Effective leaders reach out to provide the organizational support needed to set their people up for success. Their employees notice the support they get and feel obligated to give back to the organization.

Research shows that employees perform at a higher level and stay with employers when they perceive that employers value their contributions and care about their well-being. Several factors influence how supported employees feel:

1. **Fairness.** Employee perceptions of fairness by supervisors and managers has the largest impact on their feeling of being supported by the organization. Management must demonstrate fairness repeatedly before employees sense that the organization is fair. The organization needs to write fairness into its policies, distribute rewards and recognition fairly, provide timely information about policies that affect employees, and give employees a voice in decisions that affect them. Managers and supervisors need to treat employees with dignity and respect.

2. **Supervisor support.** Supervisor support follows closely behind fairness in its impact on employee perceptions of organization support. Employees see their supervisors as representatives of the organization. When they see that their supervisor supports them, they feel that the whole organization supports them. Supervisors need to be fair,

provide recognition for a job well done, and be attentive to employees' needs. This means that a little supervisory training and performance management to make sure that supervisors support their subordinates can go a long way to increasing organizational performance.

3. **Rewards and job conditions.** Employers can offer compensation, recognition, job security, promotions, training, and autonomy on the job. Interestingly, rewards by themselves have a lower impact on employees' perceptions of organizational support than fairness or supervisor support do.

Effective leaders create a culture of fairness and support, and look for ways to improve reward, recognition, job security, training, and autonomy on the job. By doing so, they get employees who are more committed to their organizations, more productive, and less likely to leave the organization — all good for the bottom line.

Create open communication

Effective leaders create an atmosphere of open and honest communication. Open communication speeds time-to-solution when problems arise. Leaders who create a defensive atmosphere don't hear about problems until too late and find themselves working at cross-purposes with their employees.

How do effective leaders create an open and honest atmosphere? First, they set the tone by listening well. They set communication ground rules for their organizations to increase constructive communication and cut down on defensive communication. They allow people to speak constructively even when the message is painful to hear.

What do supportive versus defensive communication environments look like? They differ in six ways (see Table).

Effective leaders model supportive communication behaviors and police the communication environment to make sure that people are keeping it open. They respectfully require that everyone shows respect, but not in a way that stifles honest communication. It may appear from heated debates that people are vehement about their points of view, but in an atmosphere of open communication, even those who are vehement are willing to listen to others and rebuild their perspective in response to what they hear from other people.

Table: Communication Environments

Supportive Communication Environments	Defensive Communication Environments
People describe, propose, and discuss.	People blame, attack, and defend.
People focus on describing problems and finding solutions.	People focus on controlling behavior and attitudes so that only acceptable behaviors and attitudes show up.
People speak honestly and with the intention to improve the organization.	People speak insincerely, with hidden agendas and manipulation.
People express concern for others and act out of concern for others as well as for themselves and the organization.	Communication feels impersonal or even hostile.
People treat others as equals in value and able to contribute somehow to the conversation.	Leaders communicate with their status in mind. Experts emphasize their superior skills.
People communicate to co-create their pictures of reality and of problems and solutions. Truth is a provisional thing.	People communicate to prove that they are right and others are wrong. Winners determine truth.
Source: Jack Gibb, "Defensive Communication," *The Organizational Behavior Reader*	

To ensure a supportive environment with open communication, top leaders must tame reckless managers. As mentioned earlier in this chapter, managers who harass their staff or speak so bluntly that they create an atmosphere of discomfort often regard their behavior as innocent. It isn't. Such behavior destroys open communication and creates a defensive or inhibited environment. If you do not exert control over their conduct, their behavior may pose a risk to your company. (For more on this topic, review the performance appraisals section earlier in this chapter or see chapter 6, "Mitigating Risk.")

How to Listen Actively

Good communication practices start with listening well. Communication experts have identified a few active listening behaviors that, if used in the right places, ensure that speakers feel heard and listeners actually comprehend what speakers intended. Active listening behaviors include:

1. Decide to use some or all of the active listening behaviors any time there is a possibility that you might not have understood completely something that might have been important in another person's statement.
2. Restate: "Let me see whether I understood that completely…" Restate what you think you heard.
3. Summarize: "Let me see whether I get your point. I think you're saying that…" Summarize what the other person said in your own words. Summaries are good for clarifying a large amount of information and bringing a conversation to completion.
4. Respond to nonverbal messages: "I think you're saying that…, and your smile tells me that you're excited about it."
5. Acknowledge the other person's feelings: "I think you're saying that [summarize], and that is making you angry/ frustrated/ uncertain/ excited/ optimistic/ etc."
6. Respond to the other person's feelings: "I see that you're frustrated with the situation and I'm hoping that this solution will ease your frustrations. I'm interested in your feedback once the project is complete."

Sometimes, people who are trying out active listening behaviors sound unnatural. That is understandable for any new skill. A leader can learn to use active listening behaviors by practicing in role plays until they become part of his everyday communication toolkit. But if it comes out unnaturally in a certain situation, she should try something else. Sometimes, an odd tone is a sign of discomfort with the situation or, worse, intent to manipulate. Effective leaders use active listening behaviors authentically or risk being viewed as untrustworthy.

Manage conflict constructively

Effective leaders create an atmosphere in which people discuss their conflicts and search for win-win solutions. They recognize the difference between necessary and damaging conflict. They stop unhealthy conflicts, but encourage resolution to healthy ones.

As long as there are people in organizations, there will be conflicts of interest. For instance, salespeople reach their goals when the organization promises what clients want, but staffing managers reach their goals when the organization's promises are within easy reach of what they can deliver. The issue is not whether people experience conflict, but how they work it through.

Effective leaders encourage their employees to discuss their conflicts and search for win-win solutions. This is easier when people learn to see situations from each other's perspectives and integrate what both sides see into their solutions. It also helps when parties to a conflict think of themselves as colleagues who must work together smoothly in the future. Then, it becomes more important to work out their current conflict than to prove themselves right and win the current battle.

Some conflicts are healthy. Conflicts over strategies or ways to get things done sometimes lead to creative solutions that no one thought of previously. So long as people don't take these disagreements personally, debates actually make people think harder.

Leaders who suppress all conflicts may think that they are doing their organization a favor. The conversations certainly sound more productive. But when conflicts flow underground, they simply reappear in strange ways — in sabotage, evading responsibility, holding back contributing ideas that might provoke debate, and avoiding tasks that require treading on someone else's territory. Conflict-free groups are actually less productive than groups that have healthy conflict over how to get the job done.

On the other hand, interpersonal conflicts can poison an atmosphere in a once productive office. When people take personal offense with each other, they lose their motivation to collaborate. They often start telling negative stories about each other to their other workmates, trying to get people to take their side. Effective leaders nip such conflicts in the bud.

They take people aside or bring in a professional employee relations expert to help them ease the conflict, or they remove one of the parties involved from the situation.

Effective leaders use the performance management and talent management tools mentioned in the previous sections as levers to influence the way people handle conflict. For instance, they can promote managers who have a problem-solving (win-win) perspective on conflict resolution and get coaches for managers who don't.

Value diversity

As the world becomes smaller, the workforce becomes more diverse. Leaders can turn diversity to their advantage, but first, they must see its value. Diversity is helpful to businesses facing uncertainty or change. People with diverse backgrounds can bring in new ideas. On the other hand, diversity can also result in the formation of groups that oppose each other and drag a department or company down.

When employees or managers form opinions about other people due to their title, professional background, gender, race or other demographic characteristics, they cease to view each other for their unique contributions. Communication becomes difficult. This becomes especially problematic when people form groups with opposing interests. For instance, managers and employees can become opposing camps who distrust each other. In such an atmosphere, leaders find it hard to lead because the people who are supposed to follow won't listen. Employees find it hard to give information to managers — especially negative information — because distrustful managers may punish the messenger.

Effective leaders create a greater organizational identity so that everyone in the organization sees each other as "one of us." Similarly, effective staffing firm leaders understand the diversity inherent in their contingent workforce. With both employees and contingent staff, effective leaders value diversity for the unique contributions that each person can make to the organization.

A contingent workforce is likely to be diverse, with varied motivations, attitudes and perspectives among individual workers. This mix creates an unusual challenge for supervisors who initially may assume that contingent workers are relatively homogeneous and can be managed as a single group. We now know that they aren't and can't be — at least not if you want your line managers to maximize contingent worker productivity and assignment completions.

Put simply, the best approach is to manage contingent workers on a contingent basis. No single management style or approach is likely to be equally effective for all such workers. (Actually, this is the case with most traditional workers as well.) Getting to know and managing them individually is the best way for a supervisor who must get the most out of his or her workforce.

Of course, good management practice dictates that supervisors seek to optimize all work-related situations. However, treating workers as individuals may be even more important for supervising contingent workers, among whom individual differences tend to be greater than often is the case with traditional workers. Smiling and making small talk with contingent workers will help, but it certainly isn't sufficient. The extra effort involved in engaging them in a meaningful discussion of what is important to them will pay the big dividends.

Contingent workers are especially sensitive to being treated as interchangeable "cogs" in the corporate machine. They are also surprisingly perceptive as to superficial "acknowledgements" that lack real meaning. It follows that they genuinely appreciate organizations and supervisors who make sincere efforts to get to know them as individuals.

Top managers cannot get to know everyone, but they can delegate this responsibility to frontline supervisors. Through supervisory training, leaders can develop supervisors' skills and motivation for customizing the work environment for their contingent staff.

When delegating supervisory responsibility, senior management should maintain cordial though somewhat detached relationships with the contingent workforce. In contrast, direct supervisors should get to know their contingent workers well enough to be able to customize certain aspects of the work environment to the needs and desires of these staffers. In other words, the most effective management of contingent workers ought to involve customizing their work experience to maximize those aspects of their assignment that will best motivate them to be enthusiastic and dedicated workers. This is, to be sure, an undertaking that requires management effort. The payback for this additional effort can be gratifyingly high, in the form of increased productivity, faster ramp-up (which is especially critical for contingent workers) and better knowledge transfer.

Summary

We have advocated a strategic approach to leading both tasks and people simultaneously.

By creating and communicating a compelling vision and an action plan to achieve it, leaders create futures that call employees, customers, and contingent staff to action. They make and communicate decisions effectively, knowing when to include others' input and when to go it alone. They ensure that success factors are in place when they lead organizational change. And they use change to make their organizations lean and nimble so they can pursue the visions and action plans that can make the organization great.

Through performance management, talent management, and creating a productive atmosphere, leaders can fill their firms with great people who produce great results. These strategies can be realized through the deliberate implementation of a number of programs, from selection to new hire orientation and ongoing training and leadership development, to SMART goal setting, assessment and communication of results, and well-designed systems for reward and recognition.

The most effective leaders lead by example to create a productive atmosphere. They lead with integrity and professionalism, provide organizational support to their employees, create open communication, manage conflict constructively, and work well with diversity.

Most top managers rise up through their strategic and financial abilities. But managers who lack skills for leading people usually derail or transform themselves in that arena, although there are some unfortunate exceptions. One key to leading people lies in the ability to create and manage relationships. We turn to that topic in the next chapter.

Chapter Two

BUILDING RELATIONSHIPS

Staffing firms are organizations that talk to people who agree to buy services, talk to other people who can provide those services, and get both parties to work together. They actually get paid for talking and building relationships.

Managers in highly competitive staffing firms build strong relationships with customers, contingent staff, and internal team members. Building relationships is a strategic choice. Competitive staffing firms invest in relationships with the people who make their businesses competitive now and in the future. They don't disregard the humanity of people who are not part of their success strategy, but they don't put a lot of effort into building relationships with them, either. Relationship-building takes planning and effort. Good relationship-builders use different approaches depending on their goals and on the people with whom they are connecting.

Relationship-Building Is Strategic

Competitive staffing firms develop strategic goals for their relationships with their customers, contingent staff, and internal talent. They select with whom to develop key relationships and design what those relationships should look like depending on their strategic goals and their customers' needs.

Relationship-building skills play a larger role in staffing firms' competitive advantage when they serve contingent workers or clients who have other places to go. Staffing firms must build good relationships with contingent workers in highly skilled, high-demand jobs. They must build strong relationships with large or name-brand clients, and in situations where service errors have been made, such as providing unqualified or unmotivated contingent workers who leave the client unimpressed.

Managers who built strong client relationships have salvaged countless service disasters by simply intervening quickly to rectify the situation. The strong relationship gave them the political capital needed to correct transgressions without losing the customer. High margins in competitive situations that would not otherwise justify them also depend on the quality of the relationship between staffing firm and client firm.

A large division of a Fortune 100 company placed a time-urgent order for a group of specialized IT workers that a selling branch manager had promised would not be a problem to supply. Due to a miscommunication with the supporting branch, the order got entered into the computer for the following week, causing a major production delay that was quickly visible to the corporate offices. Fortunately, a sincere explanation (and a small basket of fruit) was all that was necessary to satisfy the customer. The secret? Nothing more than a well-honed and trusting relationship between the branch manager and the customer, developed over the prior 10 months.

Relationships drive VOP success

In a VOP program, a primary supplier handles all project management for a client that needs to hire and manage many contingent workers. The primary supplier also manages all secondary suppliers of contingent staff.

The deepest relationships that staffing firms develop with customers come with these programs, which put representatives from the staffing company on site at client firms, hence the term "vendor-on-premises." These representatives gain valuable business intelligence about and respond quickly to clients' needs. In order to win and keep VOP contracts, staffing firms must be skilled at relationship-management. Relationship-building can make or break VOP success.

The staffing firm with a VOP program has the competitive advantage of gaining first-hand business intelligence and being able to respond in person. Without a VOP, the firm's managers may not hear of a problem until it becomes a three-alarm fire. At that point, damage control may take important resources away from other critical tasks.

However, even with a VOP, the staffing supplier may lose this strategic advantage if management disempowers its representative at the customer site. We discuss what it takes to empower VOP representatives in the section titled "Relationship-Building Takes Planning and Effort" later in this chapter. Insightful leaders at staffing firms whose strengths don't include building relationships might even elect to skip VOP programs and invest instead in developing other strategic advantages!

In a VOP program, three types of relationships play a role in its success. First, the relationship between VOP representative and client helps to determine the longevity of the VOP contract. Second, the relationship between staffing management and the VOP representative affects the VOP representative's probable tenure and ability to serve the client. Finally, a good relationship between staffing company management and the client can prevent the VOP representative from "going native" or being hired by a competitor, and it helps keep the VOP representative honest. Making these three kinds of relationships work takes planning and effort.

A high-volume service line may require multiple VOP reps. This calls for greater coordination among VOP representatives and between staffing firm managers and VOP reps. Jay once established a very large VOP that required 10 on-site representatives at its peak. It generated more revenue than many multi-branch staffing organizations. But it also required an extraordinary level of communication and team-building among the on-site reps and it strained the leadership skill of the on-site manager. It was like running a midsize subsidiary staffing company, all by itself.

Staffing firms' mistakes in relationship-building sometimes result in lost business. Staffing firms know how hard it is for clients to dump a supplier from a VOP. As a result, staffing firms sometimes become complacent and take the VOP program for granted. Managers can forget that many competitors knock on their clients' door on a regular basis. When competitors smell trouble, they ask questions to determine whether the relationship has become frustrating enough for the client to be willing to switch firms, despite the effort. Staffing firms that forget to keep investing in VOP relationships may discover that a competitor has prevailed.

Why would management take any relationships for granted? Because staffing firm managers may overestimate their instinct about business relationships, and the depth and tenacity of their VOP relationships. They often think that relationships are forever. They don't realize that relationships must continuously be earned. We will talk more about this later.

Keep high-quality contingents in the corral

Staffing firms that serve clients with hard-to-find workers must excel in two sets of relationships: those between managers and staffing representatives and those between staffing representatives and contingent staff. A staffing firm that doesn't take good care of its hard-to-find workers is vulnerable to having them stolen by competitors who will. These sought-after employees are more likely to exhibit prima-donna behavior. They know they are good and they love to show the world how special they are. The only thing that isn't special is having to work with them!

Although some staffing representatives take naturally to handling difficult people, most staffing representatives find it challenging to deal with such contingent workers. In staffing firms or divisions that specialize in hard-to-find workers, management must select staffing representatives for their ability to handle difficult people. In order to prevent burnout, they must find creative ways to keep staffing representatives fresh.

But what about relationships with contingent workers in high-volume operations? There just isn't time to create in-depth relationships in such a situation. Turnover is typically high among contingent staff in high-volume operations. Work assignments may be brief. And the people who turn to a staffing firm for a short-term position may not be interested in developing loyalty to the staffing firm. It makes no sense to invest in developing loyalty among such contingent workers. A staffing firm that makes such investments will not be profitable.

These contingent workers may realize that they are a dime a dozen, but they don't want to be treated as if they were! In high-volume operations, the best relationships are marked by courtesy, efficiency, and at least some effort to understand and serve each contingent worker's aspirations. When relationships are brief, people who become contingent workers choose their staffing firm based on its reputation, and often on its skills-training opportunities. A staffing firm that trains its staffing representatives to deliver consistently on expectations of courtesy and efficiency, with some concern for each contingent worker's personal goals, will develop the kind of reputation that draws skilled, reliable people to join its contingent workforce and customers who appreciate the difference.

Turnover costs and productivity

High turnover damages productivity. Losing the best employees can kill it. Building strong relationships with internal employees helps staffing firms to retain top talent and keeps all employees committed to the company's success. Relationships matter most when labor markets tighten and employees can easily find jobs elsewhere. But even during downsizing, good relationships with employees help sustain top talent. This provides a strong foundation for future growth.

Annual turnover rates in many staffing companies are in the range of 50% to 100%, a real burden for business owners. Recruiting, screening, hiring and training new workers costs a lot — tens of thousands of dollars per lost worker. Most managers know this. Then, there is the learning curve. During the first six months, many workers operate far below their potential productivity as they become acquainted with the way the firm operates. Few managers consider how turnover damages relationships. Each time a new person joins the firm, existing workers invest effort in building new relationships with that person. Constantly having to build new relationships takes away from current employees' ability to perform.

Workers with long-term relationships perform better. Consider this analogy to the airline industry: You're about to fly to Hawaii. Which crew would you prefer flying your plane: an adequately skilled pilot and crew that have worked very effectively together for several months or a highly skilled pilot and copilot who just met for the first time? Research shows that good relationships save lives. A group with experience flying together develops a rhythm of communication that allows them to give each other what the other person needs just as the other person is about to need it. Intact groups handle high-risk situations much better than fresh crews with no prior experience working together, even when the pilot is a superstar.

In staffing companies, healthy relationships can create a productive workforce. When managers develop good relationships with workers, turnover drops and productivity increases. When managers give their employees support, the employees feel as if the whole organization were giving them the support. That makes them feel obligated to contribute back to the organization. They notice opportunities to help the organization and spring into action when they see that action is needed. Good citizenship by a

47

few workers multiplies itself. They set examples for other workers, who start to feel that good citizenship is part of "the way we do things around here." They also may contribute to other workers' welfare, making them feel supported and thus obligated to do what is good for the firm.

This virtuous cycle makes for a productive atmosphere so long as the good citizenship behaviors serve to increase the organization's capacity to serve customers effectively. We don't suggest that a company becomes productive by creating a party atmosphere!

Relationships between managers and workers matter even during downsizing. During a recession, the staffing industry always suffers. Top management often cuts internal staff across the board when the going gets rough. And they often take advantage of their employees' situation by mistreating them. They forget that what goes down must come up. Staffing firms that wait for the recovery to become manifest before responding to it are destined to lose the opportunity to gain on competition. Instead, they can use the bad times to weed out poor performers and continue building relationships with high performers.

Good employees also remember the bad times. When staffing firms take advantage of bad times by ignoring their internal employees' needs, those employees jump ship as the economy improves. Conversely, when managers look out for their employees even when they don't have to, the good employees usually stay loyal when other job opportunities show up. Jay worked as second-in-command for a large regional staffing company whose owner genuinely did the right thing for his employees. During a recession, he extended support to key employees who were suffering. This included the extraordinary gesture of helping a bright young executive purchase a home. The executive reciprocated by spending years building the company with her innovative programs and boundless energy.

Why do it

There is a pot of gold at the end of the rainbow for staffing firms that excel in building good relationships. The effort must be invested where it supports both workers' long-term welfare and company strategy. High-volume providers develop brief relationships based on efficiency, courtesy, and at least some attention to each contingent worker's personal aspirations. Providers of highly skilled contingent workers specialize in building deeper relationships and display skill in handling prima donnas. During a recession, top management may have to lay off some of its workers, but it strives to keep top talent and to demonstrate its commitment to workers' welfare even when it does not have to.

Relationship-Building Takes Planning and Effort

Most people fail to realize how much planning and effort go into building and maintaining excellent relationships. Because everyone has been building relationships all of their lives, everyone believes that they are good at it. If that were the case, the courts would be virtually empty of civil lawsuits and new businesses, whose survival depend heavily on relationship-building, would flourish.

Relationships that develop by default may have qualities that aren't good for business. Worse, some people, such as the reckless managers discussed in the previous chapter, can poison the relationships between other people around them. Many managers focus on task planning and achievement and leave relationship-building to others. They ignore the quality of their people's relationships at their peril.

Managing a staffing company means managing the relationships with workers and customers. It also means monitoring and supporting relationships between VOP representatives and their customers, contingent workers, and backup suppliers, and between customer companies and contingent staff. That's a lot of relationships to handle. We offer insights into what works in each of them. Competitive staffing firms empower VOP representatives to clear away obstacles to great relationships. They select managers and workers with relationship-building skills and train them to enhance those skills further. They also avoid typical errors others make in relationships.

We start by discussing the success factors that managers should promote in relationships among people in different staffing industry roles.

Develop a network of strong relationships

Staffing companies must develop a network of relationships internal to the company and with external players. The lines of connection in this network run between staffing managers, staffing representatives, customers, backup suppliers, and contingent workers. Allowing any of these relationships to suffer is like using software with security holes in it. Some competitor will find and exploit a vulnerability, causing the company to crash like a computer afflicted with a deadly virus. For each line of connection, staffing firms must put a different set of success factors into place in order to guarantee the strength of the network.

Staffing management with VOP representatives

VOP representatives spend their time at client firms. And their success depends on serving their customers' needs. The typical VOP representative feels more a part of the client firm than the staffing firm. Successful VOP representatives sometimes "go native" if their staffing firm hasn't taken steps to make them feel that they are part of the staffing firm. Effective staffing managers touch base with their on-site representatives at least weekly — and often once or twice daily with larger programs. This not only serves to make the VOP representatives feel part of the staffing firm, but also to provide the staffing firm with vital business intelligence. VOP representatives are the first to know about customer issues that might jeopardize the customer relationship or give the staffing firm opportunities to expand services.

While this seems obvious in retrospect, it is surprising how easy it is to forget that keeping an open flow of information is the key to maintaining effective staffing programs, especially on-site programs. In a textbook example of how not to manage a VOP, a national staffing firm lost all contact with one of its on-site VOP managers. Only the branch manager communicated with this on-site VOP manager. Higher-level managers simply had too many VOPs with competing priorities demanding their time. When the branch manager left the firm, they no longer received critical information about that VOP site. The former branch manager maintained contact with the customer, even though she had switched to a competing staffing supplier. The client told her that her old company had supplied some contingent workers who were gang members. The branch manager pitched a new VOP program, with selective off-site recruiting, and won the account while retaining the on-site VOP manager, whom she had hired a few years prior. While such conduct is highly opportunistic, and probably not

Conduct Formal Business Reviews

What do smart customers and smart staffing suppliers have in common? They both insist on conducting regular business reviews, typically quarterly. Proactive staffing suppliers routinely schedule performance reviews with their larger customers without being asked.

What is so important about periodic business reviews? It is the best opportunity for the two partners in a staffing relationship to communicate with each other about the most meaningful determinants of their mutual success. In the absence of two-way communication and feedback, it is unreasonable to expect performance effectiveness to improve.

Excellent companies throughout the world are adopting quality metrics as a means of enhancing their competitive position and benchmarking their performance against similarly situated companies. It is no longer sufficient for great companies to simply "hold their own." Rather, it is expected that quality companies continue to improve each year, in relevant dimensions of performance. This can't be effectively accomplished without regular communication and feedback.

Nothing cements a relationship with a customer as much as regular communication and documentation of their effective staffing performance. Formal performance reviews memorialize the process and bestow special significance to it. Of course, it also provides an opportunity for motivated staffing suppliers to offer expanded services to their customers.

Staffing suppliers that have performed well typically want to have as many representatives from their customer, especially senior management, present for the review. This allows them to highlight their accomplishments in front of as many decision-makers and as many of their supporters as possible.

And it is a good business practice for the customer as well as for the supplier. Representatives of the customer should bring a list

continued on page 53

ethical, it highlights the importance of maintaining a close relationship with on-site managers and the vulnerability of allowing competitors in the loop.

Staffing management with customers

Successful staffing managers refresh their relationships with customers. They conduct quarterly VOP business reviews with VOP customers on all key measures of staffing performance.

The quarterly review does two things. First, it creates a discussion about what is going well, what needs to improve, and how each party can act to make the business relationship work better. Second, it gives staffing management an opportunity to prevent VOP representatives from "going native" or being hired by a competitor. Staffing managers should signal to customers how much the VOP representative is part of the staffing firm. Their relationship with the customer also prevents the VOP representative from controlling the relationship with the customer so much that he or she could take the business to a competitor.

VOP representative with the customer

A VOP representative must make the customer feel as if he/she is actually working for the customer. His/her relationship with the staffing company should almost be transparent, even though that is the VOP representative's primary employment relationship. When customers perceive the VOP representative as an extension of their own staff, they feel confident about his/her commitment to customer goals. Customers are more likely to confide in a VOP representative whose commitment is solid. Customers who trust the VOP representatives will share sensitive concerns that would otherwise go without a response — and create vulnerability for the VOP relationship in the future. This provides valuable business intelligence to the staffing firm, so staffing managers should encourage this closeness even while they monitor and build the VOP representative's loyalty to the staffing company. It's an art to manage this tension well.

Some customers are so impressed with the finesse and acumen of their on-site VOP managers that they view them as enticing recruiting prospects. While some may view this as a win-win, we regard it as a risky practice that should be discouraged. First, it confuses the roles and responsibilities of the parties. The VOP manager plays an important role as part of the staffing

continued from page 51

of questions and concerns to the review. They can use the review to understand better the subtleties of the staffing firm's process. They can learn best practices from the supplier and even learn about their own competitors' practices (but not proprietary information).

Achieve continuous improvement

Continuous improvement is the goal of all quality programs and it should be the goal of an effective business review. It is now accepted that the best companies continue to get even better every year. They may do this in a variety of ways, but an essential element is always the performance metrics that are used to track progress and quantify improvement. By setting realistic, although aggressive, performance goals — and tracking to those goals — it is amazing how much more effective and efficient organizations can become over time.

Of course, a customer cannot reasonably expect a staffing supplier to improve consistently on *all* performance metrics *simultaneously*. However, it is realistic to expect suppliers to measure and address *all* performance deficiencies promptly and to continue to improve in *some* key measures. But perhaps not the same measures consistently, and sometimes not in areas impacted by a difficult economy. There must always be some progress achieved, documented and reported.

Having an effective business and performance review facilitates greatly a company's ability to improve continuously. It is important to recognize that this is a *dual* responsibility of both the staffing supplier and the customer. It is unlikely to occur in the absence of a cooperative and candid relationship, and preferably a true *partnership*. It can never be imposed by one party upon the other. Each must be a willing participant to achieve the mutual benefits of continuous improvement.

The business review is a powerful catalyst for attaining this desired outcome. You should insist upon it and your organization should participate fully.

continued on page 55

firm. Second, the VOP manager may be good as a manager of an HR function within the client firm, but now the VOP has lost a leader with specialized knowledge about how to make the VOP serve the customer best.

We generally recommend that both the staffing firm and the customer sign mutual non-compete type agreements not to solicit or hire each others' employees, except as provided for by "liquidated damages" provisions in their contractual relationship. In fact, we have seen fees of just under $30,000 paid to the staffing firm by a customer hiring an on-site manager. In that instance, the former on-site manager participated in hiring a successor for the staffing provider as part of the transfer arrangement, and the relationship was preserved. But more typically, the departure of an effective on-site manager tends to weaken the VOP relationship and makes it more vulnerable to a competitive assault.

VOP representative with contingent staff

Excellent VOP representatives keep their best contingent workers continuously employed either at the VOP facility or elsewhere within the VOP staffing firm. This prevents excellent contingent staff from going with a competitor when the VOP vendor doesn't have an immediate assignment. VOP representatives need to make contingent workers feel as much a part of the staffing company as they feel they are a part of the customer organization. This requires that staffing firm managers make good relationships with contingent workers a priority.

Put simply, the best approach is to manage contingent workers on a contingent basis. No single management style or approach is likely to be equally effective for all such workers. (Actually, this is the case with most traditional workers as well, as we discussed in chapter 1.) Getting to know and managing them individually is the best way for a supervisor who must get the most out of his or her workforce.

Of course, good management practice dictates that supervisors seek to optimize all work-related situations. However, treating workers as individuals may be even more important for supervising contingent workers, among whom individual differences tend to be greater than often is the case with traditional workers. Smiling and making small talk with contingent workers will help, but it certainly isn't sufficient. The

continued from page 53

Formal Review Participants

Confident staffing suppliers often prefer the largest possible audience for their business reviews. It usually makes sense to invite the following individuals from the customer organization (at least initially):

1. As many end users as possible
2. As many supervisors or managers of end users as possible
3. Representatives from the customer's human resources or labor relations departments — especially if they order or specify contingent workers
4. Representatives from purchasing — especially if they negotiate the contingent workforce contract
5. The operations manager, if any
6. The EEO compliance officer, if any
7. The quality assurance manager, if any
8. The risk manager, if any
9. General management — to the degree that contingent workforce use is strategic
10. The comptroller or CFO — to the degree that contingent workforce use is substantive

While this may seem like quite a crowd to witness a contingent staffing business review, many will find it worthwhile, and the remainder will receive an educational overview and deselect themselves from subsequent meetings. Regardless, no one will lose from understanding the contingent workforce needs and processes and achievements within customer organization.

What Formal Reviews Should Cover

The most effective business reviews start with an overview of the general economy as well as the dominant service lines and niches

continued on page 57

extra effort involved in engaging them in a meaningful discussion of what is important to them will pay the big dividends.

Contingent workers are especially sensitive to being treated as interchangeable cogs in the corporate machine. They are also surprisingly perceptive as to superficial acknowledgements that lack real meaning. It follows that they genuinely appreciate organizations and supervisors who make sincere efforts to get to know them as individuals.

Senior management cannot be expected to engage a large contingent workforce in discussion directly. That is where delegation of responsibility takes over. Senior management should be genuinely interested in the welfare and motivation of its contingent workforce. Senior managers should show this interest openly and remind line managers to show their interest in individuals. Line management, in other words, should be responsible for getting to know the individual workers and monitoring their job satisfaction and their relationships with the organization that contracts for their services.

More than half a century of anecdotal evidence and empirical research support the importance of the role first-line supervision plays in the satisfaction and fulfillment of workers. For many workers the satisfaction derived from working for enlightened and caring management is more important to their job satisfaction and work motivation than salary and benefits.

VOP representative with backup suppliers

Treat backup suppliers fairly. That means not squeezing backup suppliers. A common mistake that primary suppliers make is not giving sufficient business or sufficiently profitable business to their backup suppliers. Or, the primary supplier may wait too long to give up on orders until it is too late to fill them properly or pass only the more difficult-to-fill orders to backup suppliers. This squeeze destroys their loyalty.

Disloyal backup suppliers will do the minimum necessary and may even try to push the primary supplier out of its position. Squeezing backup suppliers makes them feel exploited and less willing to provide their best candidates to the primary supplier's customer. Obviously, primary suppliers should never steal contingent staff from backup suppliers. VOPs that

continued from page 55

occupied by the particular customer. Knowledgeable customers tend to be interested in relevant labor force trends, recruiting populations and even selection ratios. The staffing firm should bring all of this information to the meeting. Reviews should include a discussion of significant problems, potential liabilities and possible areas for improvement for *both* parties to the staffing agreement. (Yes, the customer can be a major factor in the success and effectiveness of any staffing relationship.)

All business reviews should incorporate the following metrics, sometimes referred to as "key measures" in quality management programs:

1. Total dollar contingent staffing expenditures
2. Number of orders received
3. Number of orders filled
4. Average time to fill orders — and range of times
5. Number of unfilled orders
6. Number of incorrectly filled orders
7. Number of refilled orders
8. Average time to refill orders — and range of times
9. Number of cancelled orders
10. Percentages and ratios of the above-referenced metrics
11. Average time to confirm and to fill orders, by service line or by department
12. Contingent worker performance evaluation scores
13. End user satisfaction scores
14. Number of contingent workers hired on a full-time basis by the customer
15. Accidents and workers' compensation claims
16. Use of secondary or back-up staffing vendors — including similar metrics, percentages and ratios
17. Comparisons to prior reference periods and trend lines
18. Any customized metrics requested by the customer

squeeze backup suppliers develop a reputation — and not surprising — find that the best and most qualified backup suppliers will not work with them.

Minimize or eliminate any contact between potential competitors and your customer. Get the customer to agree, preferably through the VOP contract, that all backup suppliers must present to the primary supplier exclusively. Smart staffing representatives preclude competitors from calling on the customer altogether by designating the primary supplier as the exclusive interviewer of backup suppliers. Of course, being the sole point of contact for the customer obligates the primary supplier to ensure an adequate array of backup suppliers on their own or suffer the consequences. It also requires that they put effort into maintaining a strong relationship with the customer or risk losing it to one of the backup suppliers. These investments are quite worthwhile because allowing backup suppliers to develop independent relationships with the customer enables them to become future competitors.

Customers' companies with contingent staff

When staffing firms send a contingent worker to a customer site, they are choreographing the opening steps of a new relationship. Excellent staffing firms create systems to make that new relationship start smoothly. Getting other people — candidates and customers — to work well together requires some simple procedures and some wisdom.

In the atypical situation in which customer companies insist on conducting interviews prior to hiring the contingent worker, excellent staffing firms brief the customer company and the candidate with a realistic preview of the job and the candidate so there are no surprises. They get agreement up front from candidates and customers to brief the staffing firm representative immediately after the interview or first meeting and to raise any issues right away. That way, the staffing firm can troubleshoot issues before they become problems. In our experience, many issues turn out to be misperceptions that the staffing firm representative can clear up through a simple conversation. Other issues indicate a mismatch between candidate and customer. Listening to the whole story without becoming defensive enables the staffing representative to learn from his/her mistakes.

Even when the candidate and customer match well, the budding relationship can break apart due to a number of preventable or resolvable causes. Preventable causes include not knowing enough about each other or about work conditions or compensation and benefit arrangements, or logistical snafus. Most of these are easy to prevent by implementing some rather obvious procedures. Yet, some staffing firms seem to lack the imagination and foresight required to put such procedures into place. Staffing managers who forget about the human aspect of their work are blind to the need for such procedures, but most staffing managers could figure them out if pressed to do so.

Resolvable causes include starting off on the wrong foot or miscommunication. Preventing these requires a deeper level of wisdom. Here, procedures are not enough. Wise staffing representatives build a mental model of the way contingent workers operate in new work environments; this helps them understand all the ways in which relationships can go wrong even among skilled people with good intentions.

A company hiring a contingent worker is like a team bringing in a new member. The new team member must find his/her place on the team. According to Edgar Schein, an expert on team formation, new team members find themselves having to answer four questions when they join a new team:

1. What role and identity will I have on this team? Contingent workers will want to know what tasks they are supposed to take on and how those tasks fit into the overall work of the group or department. Furthermore, they want to know what social roles they will play, such as leader, follower, critic, peacemaker, life of the party, expert, new kid on the block, rebel, team hero, or just one of the guys.

2. How much control, power and influence will I have on this team? Contingent workers want to know how much of a difference their effort makes. Will they be able to pull in the resources necessary for getting the job done? Will other team members cooperate when needed? Will people listen to my ideas?

3. To what extent will my needs be met? Different contingent workers come with different needs. Some want to be paid and leave so they

can get on with the rest of their lives. Others want a sense of belonging or security along with their pay. Still others like a challenge.

4. How much will I be liked and accepted? For some people, this is a significant issue. Others concern themselves with the task and don't care too much as to whether or not they are liked.

When a contingent worker or a team member from the client firm acts in ways that indicate that there is a problem, how will you know which of the above issues is causing the odd behavior? Interestingly enough, how a person responds to a problem in one of these four areas does not indicate what the problem is. Team members typically respond in one of three ways, but how they respond says more about their personality than about the problem itself. Some respond by attacking or showing anger. Others withdraw from the situation or stifle themselves. Still others reach out to show too much caring and concern. Whatever their response, wise staffing representatives know that these behaviors are responses to an underlying issue. They ask questions to discover the underlying issue from the contingent worker's perspective and the team members' perspective rather than making assumptions.

In low-volume service lines, staffing representatives can take the time to develop a sense for individual contingent workers' needs in regard to the above four questions. In high-volume service lines, there usually isn't time for that and staffing representatives have to find out only when something goes wrong. Especially in high-volume service lines, VOP managers should create procedures that make it easy for contingent workers to give them timely and honest feedback about how things are going — beyond the obvious metrics.

Empower VOP representatives

Competitive staffing firms that use VOP empower their VOP representatives to clear obstacles to great relationships. For instance, managers may not have communication channels for their VOP representatives to raise red flags, or they may not have trained their VOP representatives to distinguish between problems they should handle on their own versus problems that require calling for backup. Worse, managers who respond to problems by blaming subordinates instead of starting with collaborative problem solving may scare subordinates into hiding problems until they get out of control.

Consider the following scenario. A staffing firm had a good relationship with its VOP customer, a food services company. The customer was planning to hire another staffing provider for a new light industrial service line that it did not think the original staffing firm had the expertise to handle. The company planned to put the new service line up for bid with specialty firms that would have provided computerized time clocks and the procedures for their use. However, the talented VOP manager, who had the confidence of her senior management at the branch office level, felt sufficiently empowered to purchase a computerized time clock system quickly, before the client had a chance to put the new service line out for bid. This initiative by the VOP manager so impressed the customer that she was given an opportunity to demonstrate whether her VOP could "stretch" to this new service line. It turned out that it could — and her firm still controls the account.

Staffing managers want a VOP program to be relatively self-sufficient. On the other hand, they want their VOP representatives to raise issues that they cannot resolve themselves. Part of the art of creating a strong relationship between management and VOP representatives lies in managing this tension well.

Staffing managers should treat a VOP representative the same way they treat any operating unit. First, they should provide VOP representatives with the resources to solve problems on their own. This reduces the demand on managers' time. It also enables VOP representatives to serve their customers quickly, confidently, and smoothly. Second, they need to create an open communication environment for "penalty-free" communication. (We discussed what it takes to create such an environment in chapter 1.)

Staffing managers should also create an open communication environment where VOP representatives can report problems that look as if they might be bigger than they can handle. Managers should encourage VOP representatives to feed information about problems through channels as soon as they see that they may not be able to resolve the problem themselves. Without such open communication, managers are blind to issues that could cause customer turnover. In a defensive communication environment, VOP representatives worry that they will be blamed for problems and thus feel the need to conceal evidence of problems from their managers. (See Chapter 1.)

Even when managers promote an open communication environment, power differences may provide VOP representatives with a powerful incentive to conceal problems. Top managers often have strong personal relationships with the largest customers. In order to look good in front of top managers, VOP representatives sometimes pretend that all is well with those customers. This creates a perverse situation where the upward flow of reliable information is weakest with the most valuable customers.

Given their power, top managers need to offer more permission and offer it more often than lower-level managers. Top managers can use their relationships with customers to assuage customers when things don't go well. They need to offer this help to VOP representatives without strings attached or negative judgment. When top managers deliver the message, "I'm here to help you give our customer excellent service," they build VOP representatives' commitment to communicating openly.

Seek and develop relationship-building skills

The more that relationship-building skills give a company its competitive advantage, the more the firm must recruit employees with those skills. A solid recruiting program and selection system prepares the company to be competitive. Staffing firms can also train their employees in understanding diverse people, communication, interpersonal influence, conflict resolution, negotiation, working with difficult people, and other relationship-building skills.

Use validated assessment methods

Staffing firms often assume that people who interview well for a job will be good at doing the job. Most hiring managers have an inflated perception of the utility of interviews for selecting effective employees. Research shows that interviews don't do a good job of assessing many critical skills necessary for job performance. Interviews are an artificial form of conversation. To succeed in a typical interview, people have to do things that would not be appropriate in other circumstances.

Staffing firms may wish to borrow proven methods from other industries. For instance, some companies put sales candidates through simulations or role-playing exercises to assess their ability to develop new business by building relationships. This assesses conversational skills, general sales skills, customer-focus, and product knowledge.

Staffing firms can also purchase validated tests to assess skills and abilities, including social skills and, perhaps in the future, "emotional intelligence." However, users should be cautious to ensure that the tests they purchase have been professionally developed and validated. This means that the tests have been put through a process that shows how well test scores correlate with success on the job for which they will be used. In a typical test-validation process, people who are already in the job take the test, and so do people who are in jobs that differ significantly. In order for the test to be valid, people in the focal job must score higher on the test than people in different jobs. Even better, a pool of people is tested before they take on the focal job, and test scores predict the level of job performance as measured months later. A test that predicts future job performance is considered valid.

Many testing companies sell assessments that have not been proven to predict job performance — and may in fact be discriminatory. In some cases, the evidence of validity was collected for jobs other than the one a staffing company is hiring for. The courts consider this an improper use of the test. Using a test to screen for a job for which there is no evidence of test validity exposes a company to lawsuits by people who were rejected for the job based on their test scores. We discuss this further in chapter 6.

Unlike tests, role plays that mimic real job situations and call on candidates to behave the way they will be expected to behave on the job are taken to be valid screening devices. Good instructional designers or screenwriters can be hired to create the role-play situations. Sometimes experienced job incumbents who are creative writers can be called upon to produce role-play materials. Role-plays are cheap to produce, but expensive to use. They require one or more employees to act out the script and at least one employee with a sharp eye, to both observe and evaluate the candidate's behavior. In most cases, companies use one employee to do both, but this works only when the employee doesn't have to think much in order to play the role.

Develop and enhance the skills

Once people are hired who have relationship-building skills, staffing firms can develop those skills further through training. They can even use training to implement consistent communication procedures that become part of the organization's way of doing business. When customers and contingent workers see the consistency of these procedures, strength in building relationships becomes part of the firm's brand image.

Effective training in communication and relationship-building goes beyond piling knowledge into employees' brains. Effective training gets people to produce new behaviors. It also gives them feedback and chances to improve on their first try. The best feedback describes behaviors that helped and behaviors that hindered performance. When choosing a training program, leaders should ask how much actual practice and how much feedback on that practice trainees will get during training. They should also ensure that trainees will get feedback on those new behaviors while on the job. Otherwise, what was learned in the classroom disappears from the employee's repertoire. Observation and feedback can be done by an expert trainer or by an employee's supervisor. Computer-based training can be used to provide examples of good and bad relationship-building behavior, but it cannot substitute for repeated practice and feedback in simulations or on the job.

In order to reinforce the results of training programs, supervisors and managers should receive the same training that their employees receive, or at least an overview combined with training on how to observe employees' behavior and give feedback. Managers should also learn how to manage relationships for results and how to manage their employees' relationships. Good leaders learn about their impact on the quality of others' relationships and learn how to expand their communication skills to be able to have the right impact.

While choosing a training program, leaders can develop criteria by which they will deem the training program a success. They should consider five levels of criteria, but focus mostly on which behaviors should be taught. The first level is trainees' reactions to the training itself. That includes feeling that the training was worthwhile, and — most important — committing to use the new behaviors on the job. The second level is trainees' ability to understand the material and use the new behaviors during the training session. Tests or role-plays with feedback can be used to assess the second level. The third level is trainees' use of new knowledge and behaviors on the job. Supervisors, outside observers, and even customers can rate how well trainees are implementing the new behaviors. The staffing firm can give customers customer satisfaction surveys that ask the customer to rate the extent to which a specific employee used behaviors that they learned during training. The fourth level is business results. This can include number of new customers retained, customer satisfaction ratings, sales volume, sales dollars, number of contingent workers placed, etc. The fifth level is return on investment. A simple cost-benefit calculation will suffice.

Leaders in staffing firms whose strategies require building relationships should develop selection and training programs to produce a cadre of employees with strong relationship-building skills. They should evaluate their selection and training programs to keep improving them or to know when to replace them with something better.

What are relationship-building skills?

What skills do people need to build good relationships? Good relationship-builders in the business world operate with two compasses: their business goals and other people's needs and aspirations. They cater to both creatively.

Relationships can be seen as a system of give-and-take. Good relationship-builders understand how to discover what other parties want most and find ways to contribute those things without incurring significant costs. Employers and employees act as if there were an implied contract specifying what each party will contribute to the situation. Relationships break down when one or more parties feel that they can no longer trust the other to contribute their part of the bargain or, worse, when they come to expect that the other person will do them harm. Relationships become especially powerful when one or both parties contribute something that multiplies the other person's power or contribute something unexpectedly good. For instance, employees can accomplish a great deal in ways that make their bosses get promoted more quickly.

Contributing what others will value

What can people contribute that builds a relationship? Effective relationship-builders learn to recognize what their relationship partners will value, especially what their relationship partners cannot obtain from other sources. For instance, in a staffing firm of mostly non-engineers placing technical staff, a former engineer can see consequences of placement choices much more clearly than non-engineers can. He or she will know when a specific skill requirement that the customer says is important is truly critical. When a customer assumes certain skill requirements without stating them, the engineer will know what they are. In a high-volume service line placing contingent workers with a difficult manager, a recruiter with unusually good intuition about people will be able to distinguish between contingent workers who will be able to handle the difficult manager and those who will be eaten alive.

Effective relationship-builders in a business context are able to weigh the benefits and the costs of satisfying other people's wants and needs and be able to say "no" in a palatable way. This is especially important when dealing with demanding customers or hard-to-find contingent workers. Contingent divas know that they have skills that customers cannot obtain elsewhere and may use their leverage to try to extract unreasonable benefits. Saying "no" in a palatable way takes some creativity.

Jonathan once worked with a customer whose organization missed several project deadlines, raising project management costs to a painful level: "We had to reduce what we delivered or cut significantly into our margins. Before telling the customer that we proposed making some reductions, our project team brainstormed ways that we could improve the final product even while we reduced our costs. When we spoke to the customer, we presented the whole package of reductions and improvements as an overall benefit to the client. The client accepted our proposal and even sped up their own work on the project. Strong communication skills and commitments to our needs and to our client's needs made this possible."

Demonstrating empathy

So far, this discussion of relationship-building skills sounds like a cost-benefit analysis combined with a creative approach to finding benefits for all parties in a relationship. But effective relationship-builders also develop emotional skills. The first is empathy. That means standing in other people's shoes to see what they see and imagine what they feel. It also means feeling genuine concern for another person's well-being. Effective relationship-builders understand and care about other people even while they make business decisions about what they can and cannot contribute to others. Without empathy, managers find it hard to comprehend what another person will experience as a benefit. Without empathy, managers often respond to a problem by blaming others, which alienates the very people who can solve the problem.

Empathy can improve a manager's ability to motivate others. Employees distrust managers who cannot see situations from their point of view or who don't care to give them support. Managers who lack empathy often find that their workers respond in kind, making only a half-hearted effort toward achieving the manager's business goals. Such managers tend to rely on financial incentives or fear to drive their workers to comply with their demands. The former is expensive and the latter is a toxin that weakens an organization in the long run.

In contrast, empathetic managers keep an eye on helping employees achieve their aspirations, which make the employees committed to helping the manager achieve his or her goals. Such managers often find it easy to motivate their workers to achieve the organization's goals. They also find that clients are more likely to forgive their mistakes when things go wrong. When a manager lacks empathy, clients are more likely to blame problems on the manager's lack of concern. Conversely, an empathetic manager's clients are more likely to blame circumstances and give the manager a chance to recover.

Repairing damaged relationships

When things go wrong, rebuilding trust becomes a critical relationship-building skill. Trust develops when people feel that their relationship partner has their own best interests in mind and are willing and able to deliver on their end of the bargain. Everyone knows that trust breaks down when one or both parties becomes less trustworthy. When one party cannot or will not keep their side of the bargain, the other party loses faith in them. But also, trust breaks down when one or both becomes less trusting.

Not being trusting means not letting the other person have a chance to prove that they will deliver their part of the bargain. It is fashionable in some sectors of the business world for managers to show off their paranoia. While that works well to guard against competitors, it kills off relationships with collaborators and clients. A manager who isn't trusting will impose demands on the people around him or her, alienating them and making them less trusting, in return.

To repair a broken relationship, all parties must demonstrate that they are both trusting and trustworthy. Achieving this can happen in several steps:

1. Each person admits that there is a problem with the relationship and commit to resolving it. One way to accomplish this is to describe what they want from a healthy relationship and what they are willing to give, and then to commit to bringing about that healthy relationship. Without such a commitment, no one will take action. Each party must realize that this process will require work and may be painful.

2. Each person tells his or her story about what worked with the relationship and what happened that broke the trust. Then he or she describes what a healthy relationship would look like. Listen to the other person tell his or her story without commenting or defending.

3. Say what the other person could do that would show that they are trustworthy.

4. Take actions that demonstrate trustworthiness. This simply means making promises to deliver what the other party wants or needs and following through on them.

5. Try being trusting. This means giving the other person a chance to take action that demonstrates trustworthiness. This requires being vulnerable to the other person's intentions or ability to follow through. In a truly dangerous situation, one should try being trusting on safe issues, first, and build on the sense of trust that this creates. For instance, nations at war usually shift to a cold peace based on promises and surveillance to determine how well the other country follows through. They don't become allies right away.

6. When one party falls down on a commitment, trust is repaired most quickly when two things happen. First, the person who failed to deliver takes responsibility and promises to deliver what was promised or promises to deliver the next time the opportunity arises. Second, the other person forgives but reminds the first party that following through the next time is important.

7. Build on trust by making and keeping larger and larger promises until both parties depend on each other and know that the other person has their back.

Sometimes, people cannot take these steps on their own. They need a mediator. If both parties believe that the other person is the problem and that the other person will not change, a mediator can be brought in to work some magic. The mediator leads both parties through the steps just discussed. For instance, the mediator asks each person what the other party could do that would persuade them that the other party might be trusted a little. The mediator gets each party to agree to take some symbolic action that acts as a signal to the other party that things have changed for the better. A manager can act as a mediator between employees, between a staffing representative and a client, or between a contingent worker and a client. Effective staffing companies usually have someone with strong mediation skills in a respected position or hire a consultant with strong communication skills to act as a neutral party.

Why can't people easily solve such a problem on their own? Because people deceive themselves. It's amazing how deeply people come to believe the stories they tell themselves about another person's supposedly horrible intentions. The stories become self-fulfilling prophecies. First, the stories cause them to make accusations that undermine trust and destroy the relationship. Usually, the person telling the story is blind to his or her contribution to the destruction of the relationship. We have heard some unbelievable stories told about good people. And we have watched good people go to war with each other unnecessarily.

Which of these skills can be developed in existing staff? Skills that cannot be developed should become criteria for selecting new staff.

Communication skills and commitment to others' well-being can be learned through training, coaching, mentorship, and from role models. Bringing in a CEO or another influential leader with strong communication skills and commitment to clients and employees can inspire others to emulate the strong leader. However, even in that situation, many people believe that the leader has special skills and cannot see their way to growing such skills themselves. Training or coaching followed up by regular feedback helps ensure that people actually develop the skills.

Empathy may be more innate. Studies of autistic people have convinced some researchers that such people simply cannot imagine what another person thinks or feels, as if that part of their brain were damaged. Normal people vary from mildly empathetic at times to very empathetic all of the time. On the low end of the scale, we have seen examples of managers whose careers were derailed by a lack of empathy who somehow dug deep inside to find whatever empathy they had and nurtured it. These managers all faced a huge crisis and had a trusted coach or mentor who helped them see that their career would fall into a hole if they didn't develop their empathy. Even more difficult, the coaches and mentors put the managers through a painful process that many people would not be willing to undergo.

In one case, a manager who was a slave driver was promoted repeatedly because she could turn around crisis situations. She was sent to one failing operation after another. In each case, employees lacked motivation and a sense of direction. Broken systems and broken trust paralyzed each operation. Her vision, decisiveness and grit saved the day. Then, she was promoted to a vice presidential position whose success was based on influence skills. She continued to act like a commanding officer because that is what she knew how to do. But now, the people she communicated with were highly skilled, highly motivated professionals who resented her abrasive style.

They felt that she didn't trust them. She didn't bother trying to understand their needs. She didn't notice how committed they were to the success of the business. And she couldn't even see how resentful they felt about her inappropriate behavior. A masterful coach put a mirror to her so she could see how she looked to others. How alienating she was came as a shock to her. At one point, she broke down in tears and apologized publicly for her behavior. Her public statements won other people's sympathy, and they assisted her in changing her style.

Note, though, that this manager was unusual. Most managers whose careers are undermined by a lack of empathy would probably let their careers falter rather than experience such a humiliating process. A good consultant with executive coaching skills lives for this kind of breakthrough with their clients. But they are rare because most managers aren't ready for the sometimes gut-wrenching inner work and not many consultants have the skills to guide a client who is ready. Most people never get to the point of being ready for such breakthroughs because they fail to recognize or take responsibility for the results of their relationships. Several common errors cause this failure.

Preventing typical errors in relationships

People are prone to certain kinds of errors in relationships. The first we already described — deceiving ourselves with stories we tell about other people. That phenomenon often is based on a string of errors.

This sequence is easiest to see when something goes wrong. Because they don't look in mirrors very often, people tend to see what is going on around them rather than seeing themselves. When something goes wrong, they tend to blame circumstances and the other people involved. This leads to playing the blame game in a lot of business relationships. Worse, because they cannot peer into another person's mind, it's harder for them to make sense of his or her actions.

They worry that the other person has bad intentions. Furthermore, they tend to explain the other person's behaviors as reflecting negative personality traits. Then, they relate to the other person as a bad person, which makes it very difficult to repair the relationship. The steps to repairing trust in a relationship may look simple, but they are very difficult when this string of errors has occurred, which is all too often.

Curtail the blame game

Damaged relationships don't get repaired until at least one person is willing to empathize with and forgive the other person. Some managers are too focused on tasks to be empathetic or forgiving. So they easily jump to conclusions that a certain employee is a bad apple after something goes wrong. Managers like this may put constraints on the employee or let them go when the worker was perfectly capable of doing better.

How can managers get around their natural inclinations to play the blame game and to misjudge other people? One branch manager, for example, excelled at turning new sales staff into successes, even if they failed at first. He knew how easy it was to give up on people and employed a few strategies to fight that tendency.

First, he listened carefully to new employees' explanations for why they failed at something. He liked to hear people saying that they were responsible and would do better the next time. This gave him an opening to give the new worker some training at exactly the time when he or she was most open to learning from it. He also liked to hear people saying that they failed because of a poor strategy or a lack of effort. That person was likely to learn new strategies and put out more effort than someone who blamed their failure on lack of ability or bad luck. In contrast, people who feel that lack of ability causes their failures are likely to give up. And people who blame bad luck have no reason to put out more effort or change their strategies.

Second, he worked to persuade people that having good strategies and putting out a lot of effort would produce success. He told stories about superstars' early struggles to succeed. This gave new employees hope that they could become as good as the best salespeople in the company.

Third, he tested people's ability rather than assuming that a lack of ability was at the root of a failed deal. Managers who worked for him would routinely say, "I don't think that New Employee X has what it takes to succeed." He would ask, "How do you know? Have you identified what they are doing wrong and worked with them to improve their skills?"

Finally, he gave training to everyone. He had tapes for every critical skill and tapes to improve people's motivation and hunger for success. He called in the company trainer often to sit in on sales calls and work with people on their skills. When a new employee did not respond to training, he would give up. But not before that.

He also did these things with himself. He took responsibility for the success of his office and went for training himself. He acted as a role model. As a result of these strategies, he turned around an office known as "the morgue" into the company's flagship operation. Interestingly, relationships in that office were good among all the people, not just between the general manager and the workers he believed in. Workers in other offices played the blame game often, but rarely in his.

Finding ways to curtail the blame game can have a huge impact on business success.

Allow relationships to change when circumstances change

There are other errors worth preventing, as well. First, people forget that relationships change when circumstances change. People need to be prepared for the changes. Sometimes, they need a way to give up the old relationship and to embrace a new one. Giving up a cherished relationship makes people feel a sense of loss. When something important was lost, people actually need a chance to grieve for their loss.

When a person gets promoted from a peer to a supervisor, the new supervisor and the former peers often act just as friendly as they did before. However, when the supervisor has to keep an employee accountable for the first time, this new behavior comes as a shock. New supervisors who aren't well-prepared for this often feel as if their friends are abandoning them. Peers who aren't well-prepared for this may feel that there is something wrong with their old friend. They become resentful of this cold new person.

A team of three talented consultants who had worked together as friends in the IT placement business left their company to start a new technical service division for a large regional staffing service. Because there was no IT head in place at their new employer, one of the three had to assume the leadership role. For the first time, they were no longer peers. The most productive of the three quickly refused to assume the leadership role, fearing that it would result in a significant loss of personal income. Everyone seemed in agreement as to which of the remaining two colleagues should take charge.

But it was leadership in name only. The new leader was unwilling to actually manage his friends, and instead let them each do their own thing, as they had done in the past. Not enough new business was being generated and the operation began to fail. The most productive consultant elected to leave first. Management at the regional staffing firm was embroiled in political battle and unable to respond effectively. The operation limped along for a while and then disappeared.

Manage relationships during organizational change

Similarly, organizational change can play havoc with established relationships. Leaders make a huge error in believing that once they have taken the time to plan organizational change, all their followers need do is to work the plan. This is a recipe for disaster; most organizational change efforts fail to meet their targets because leaders fail to plan time and processes for people to rework their relationships. Restructuring pulls people apart and puts new people together. It takes work to establish new relationships. Worse, people often feel resentful about having to go through the change and take it out on the new people they have to work with. They often engage in passive-aggressive behavior, take their sweet time to return phone calls, ignore budget constraints, provide their new business relationship partners with half-baked deliverables, or get angry very easily.

William Bridges, in his seminal book *Managing Transitions*, talks about the need to formally address transitions that people experience during organizational change — to make endings and new beginnings official and to provide time for people to muddle through the "neutral zone" between the old and the new. He notes that people go through a stage between letting go of old things and new beginnings where people feel anger, loss and confusion. Leaders need to help people manage this transition. In an informal or creative culture, leaders might hold a ceremony to discard old symbols and create new ones. In a more formal culture, the CEO might give a speech and send around a marketing video about the organization's bright new future. In either case, people need someone to talk with or some experience to go through in order to let go of the old order and handle their emotional reactions to change. They also need time to get used to the new ways of doing things and processes for working out the details of the change.

Many years ago, when desktop PCs were new, Jonathan managed a group that had to shift to new processes backed by computers. The staff had no computer experience. Most were afraid of the new way of doing things. Some workers felt that they could not succeed with the new processes. This continued even as a couple of early adopters actually improved their results and enjoyed their work more. "Although we listened to people's concerns, we thought that informing them about how things would work was all they needed. We had no idea how entrenched their worries were. Instead of giving them time to stew about it, we put pressure on them to perform. Some left the organization, and we lost some good people. Had we given them some exercises in which they would experience the new system as friendly, some discussions where they could process their feelings without our disagreeing with them and trying to persuade them that things would be OK, and relaxed our performance standards for a few days, they might have stayed and thrived like the other workers."

Nurture constructive dissent

A less common error is called "The Abilene Paradox," a term coined by Jerry Harvey, a management professor. In an Abilene Paradox, people publicly agree to something that they actually disagree with privately. This happens when people imagine that bad things will happen if they say what they think. For instance, their boss will fire them or their peers will reject them. The agreements that people make under these circumstances often turn out to be mistakes. After things go wrong, people protect themselves by trying to assign the blame to others.

In some cases, people discover that they were not the only ones who privately disagreed with the decision. Sometimes they can even laugh about it. But when their thoughts stay secret, rifts build between people. The only solution is for someone to have the courage to state his or her true thoughts. This is easier in an environment of open communication, but even then, it requires courage. In a defensive communication environment, people's hidden agendas stay secret, and the blame game creates rifts that fester.

In all of these situations, solutions to problems in relationships are usually impossible without open communication environments and wise leaders. Most organizations lack the openness to overcome blame games. Few leaders have the wisdom to question their own biases about other people's motivations or to know how to lead people through the mental and emotional transitions required for successful change efforts. Organizations that achieve superior results over decades usually build great relationships from a foundation of open communication and wisdom about relationships.

Chapter Three

PROVIDING SERVICES

Highly competitive staffing firms solve the dilemma between "the customer is always right" and "we're in business to make money." They provide customers with what they can afford in creative ways that deliver what the customers need. What customers say that they want is not always the same as what they need. In order to be creative, staffing firms must understand client company strategy and operations.

The best staffing firms get to know their customers' staffing requirements for meeting the demands of the market. Staffing firms must build their strengths to match their customers' priorities for speed, price, quality, or customer service. Staffing services designed to match those priorities keep customers coming back for more. In this chapter, we discuss the basics of strategy and expand on those basics in the next chapter on marketing and branding.

Most competitive staffing firms use vendor-on-premises (VOP) programs to deliver their mix of services. VOP programs reduce customer costs by cutting the number of vendors the customer must coordinate with. VOPs enable staffing firms to develop close relationships with customers. This gives them access to vital business intelligence and allows them to control the flow of staffing services to the customer. Running a VOP program effectively is an art. In this chapter, we discuss how this can be done well. We also discuss several service options in human resources, 24/7 customer service, ancillary services, backup recruitment, business review and reporting.

Competitive staffing firms keep ahead of the curve in providing human resources services — either as add-ons or to increase contingent worker quality. The best staffing firms emphasize training. They use it strategically, where it makes them most competitive in helping customers meet the demands of the market. In this chapter, we discuss what training to provide, when to provide it, and how to use best practices in designing and evaluating training. Competitive staffing firms also employ skills assessment and psychological testing programs as well as background checks and references to improve the match between contingent workers and customers.

Finally, competitive staffing firms structure themselves to provide services most effectively. We discuss how to maximize performance by keeping sales and service separate.

Align Services with Customers' Real Priorities

Customers often demand impossible speed or low prices, and then they discover their staffing firms providing them with low quality. The best staffing firms understand and make it clear to their customers which one or two benefits they can provide better than other firms — speed, price, quality, or customer service. And they match the benefits with the client's greatest needs. They provide what customers truly need, not simply what they ask for.

When customers are asked what they expect of their staffing providers, they generally say "qualified people at the lowest rates, delivered tomorrow." But customers tend to overemphasize the importance of low rates when they think of hiring temporary workers as if they were buying a commodity. They expect staffing firms to find this commodity at increasingly lower rates, especially as volume goes up. They create competition among service providers to source large numbers of mediocre workers.

This works with high volume accounts where workers' skill sets are a commodity, such as light industrial workers. If all a company needs is a semi-skilled worker to stand at a machine at an assembly line, it doesn't need selection finesse from the staffing provider. The more sophisticated and hard-to-find skill sets don't work like this. Pressing staffing providers for lower rates for sophisticated workers doesn't make sense because they are difficult to recruit. When pressed for lower rates, staffing providers will send scarce workers to their higher-paying, more elite customers to increase their margins, leaving the less-skilled workers for the company that is pressing for the lower rates.

Avoid the squeeze

When companies squeeze their suppliers for harder-to-find workers, they get poor quality workers, if they get any at all. However, if the customer is large enough, the staffing firm may elect to take a small loss on a few higher-quality workers in hard-to-fill categories in order to protect the overall business relationship. This works only to a point. When customers keep asking for more and more of the hard-to-find workers at a discounted rate, staffing firms start to feel the losses. Smart staffing suppliers balk when the losses from searching for hard-to-find workers eat into the profits from the overall order.

In this situation, the supplier's incentive becomes to save those workers for smaller customers that are willing to pay "retail rates." A large customer may protect itself in this scenario by holding the staffing firm accountable for performance metrics such that it is readily apparent if the staffing firm is not supplying an adequate number of qualified workers in a timely fashion. When it becomes apparent that a customer might need a significant number of hard-to-find workers, staffing firms can negotiate an increased gross profit margin for those orders.

Some customers ask staffing firms to send workers immediately. That may be a true priority sometimes, but often the rush is because the customer needlessly waited until the last moment to place orders. Competitive staffing firms educate their customers to see the unreasonable load that last-minute orders create and the downward spiral of worker quality that occurs with a last-minute order.

The faster the order must be filled, the lower the quality and performance of the workers that are likely to be found quickly. Many of those workers represent the "bottom of the barrel" — people who have not been able to secure assignments elsewhere. Sometimes, a candid conversation with a customer is all that it takes to break this destructive and burdensome habit in which both the staffing company is overwhelmed by hard-to-fill orders at "closing time" and the customer is forced to accept whomever is available at the last moment.

To get a good view of these tradeoffs, it's best to step back and look at why customers need staffing firms. First, customers whose work happens as projects cannot hire and release large numbers of workers without high unemployment insurance, high recruiting costs, and damage to workers' loyalty. Staffing firms have done much of the recruiting ahead of time, spreading recruiting costs over a series of projects. They find each worker a series of short-term jobs.

This enables each customer to get the work done without keeping the worker around longer than necessary, yet keeps the workers loyal to each job because they know there is likely to be another one just around the corner. For a customer that needs a large number or workers for the short-term, getting workers who will be effective despite being on board for only a short period is worth it, even if those workers have solid, but not stellar skills.

When a customer needs a large number of workers and their quality is not an issue, then they can demand a lower price. For instance, a light manufacturing company may need to fill an unusually large order. The company can bring on a large number of semi-skilled workers to do simple tasks until the order is completed.

Second, as the global economy speeds up, projects must be ramped up more quickly and their work completed more rapidly. Customers need a pool of labor ready to jump in when a project starts. This need is so acute when it comes to cutting-edge skills that they are willing to pay more for a contingent worker with hard-to-find skills than they would for a long-term professional. For instance, a company may be rewarded with millions or even hundreds of millions of dollars in sales revenue by beating competitors to market with a highly prized product. Spending extra money to secure the skilled staff needed to win that race provides a huge payoff. For such a customer, quality is the top priority, with speed a close second.

The best staffing firms understand their customers' strategic imperatives. For what accomplishments does the market reward this customer? For being first to market with something simple or with something that has never existed before? For filling large, simple orders quickly? Or for getting everything just right no matter how long it takes?

The best staffing firms also understand their customers' staffing imperatives. What kind of staffing is needed to make the strategy work? Factors in this equation include skill level, the difficulty of finding people with those skills, the length of lead time available, the duration of the project, and the extra value added by securing people with the right skills at the right speed.

Those strategic and staffing imperatives determine the customer's need for contingent staff and what services staffing firms should provide. The best staffing firms supply what customers truly need, not simply what they ask for.

Deliver vendor-on-premises programs

In their search for the right mix of speed, price and quality, customers often centralize their contingent workforce procurement function to bring order to an often chaotic process. Lacking centralization, hiring managers would negotiate their own contracts with different staffing firms. All that negotiation takes time and effort. Worse, hiring managers pay unnecessarily high bill rates. Sometimes, a high-level manager would set a cap on bill rates so low that the company would be limited to hiring the worst contingent workers. With centralized procurement, a customer can offer larger contracts to staffing firms, making it worthwhile to a staffing firm to offer lower rates.

Two forms of centralization have been developed: Software companies have developed vendor management system (VMS) software to track staffing suppliers. That puts control of the staffing function in the customer's hands. A staffing firm may offer to do the centralization for the customer and place a representative on the customer's premises. This is called a vendor-on-premises (VOP) program.

Customers like VOP programs because they typically result in lower-price markups, higher quality service, and fewer vendors to deal with. Staffing firms like them because they can provide as much profit as non-VOP business while shielding them from competitors. However, VOP programs must be executed well in order to avoid problems. In order to win and keep VOP contracts, staffing firms must prove that they are skilled at relationship management. And VOPs may not even be the best solution in some situations.

VOP representatives gain valuable business intelligence about and respond quickly to clients' needs. But how large a staff is required to support a VOP?

VOP best practices

Following are best practices and signs of a well-run VOP program.

- Reviews and reporting. The staffing firm running the VOP provides a quarterly business review meeting with key customer representatives.
- Problem-solving. The VOP representative uses relationships to gather business intelligence on problems and opportunities within the customer's organization. This enables the staffing firm to be proactive in several ways.
  - The VOP representative brings problems to the customer's attention and preferably provides solutions — before the customer has to bring problems to the VOP representative's attention. Self-diagnostic and corrective performance mechanisms should be in place.
  - The VOP representative anticipates customer staffing needs and brings them to the customer before any deficiency becomes obvious. Excellent operators are always proactive and rarely caught off guard.
  - When the rare problem emerges that the VOP provider did not detect first, they quickly accept responsibility, avoid defensiveness, fix the problem, figure out how to avoid its repetition, and let their customers know what went wrong and why.
- Comfortable process. The staffing firm's process makes both the contingent workers and the traditional workforce feel comfortable. Everyone feels needed and communication flows easily. The staffing process should be transparent to all parties.
- Communication between customer and backup providers. The VOP provider manages communication between the customer and backup providers, but does not try to squelch it. The VOP representative uses the trusting relationship he/she has with the customer to learn from the customer about best practices of the competing staffing firms.

- Active listening. The VOP representative listens to the customer's management and supervisory teams and responds to them. Their needs must be served better with the VOP program than without it.
- Relationship building. The VOP representative builds relationships and provides services consistently well, so that contingent staff, the traditional workforce, and the customer organization's management make no complaints about, or around, the VOP provider.
- Quality staff selection. The VOP representative selects contingent staff well enough and troubleshoots problems with staff quickly enough that the customer brings no administrative complaints or charges relating to workers supplied by the VOP provider.

Most VOP programs require full-time staff supplied by the primary vendor in order to function. But the number of the staff members ranges from one individual (perhaps even part-time), to as many as 10 or 12 in very large programs. The number of such individuals supplied as part of the VOP program is somewhat discretionary and subject to negotiation. It inevitably affects the level of service.

Sometimes it is not merely a function of determining the minimal number of the individuals necessary to support the program, but also of incorporating extra capacity that can be used to support and service the existing non-contingent workforce. Most VOP providers recognize that their on-site coordinators have significant downtime after workers are dispatched and checked in. The challenge is to exploit that time to provide additional, productive services.

The downtime is typically used to strengthen the relationship with individual end-users at the customer site, as well as to troubleshoot any problems and to recruit and interview future workers. It can also be used to support other functions for the staffing supplier, such as telemarketing for new business outside of the customer organization with the customer's permission. But using that downtime to provide services that makes the customer ever more dependent on the staffing firm helps cement the relationship and provides more channels through which the

VOP representatives can gather business intelligence about the customer organization, thus allowing them to become more proactive over time.

Staffing firms that provide VOP programs can build their margins by providing optional add-on services in human resources, 24/7 service options, and ancillary services. The best time to optimize the VOP program is precisely while negotiating conditions with the customer. However, sales representatives are sometimes so excited at having landed a VOP contract, they forget to negotiate such add-on services, and customers often don't know what additional services to ask for.

VOP Worst Practices

Following are the worst practices of a VOP program and signs that something is wrong.

- Little or no communication. VOP managers don't initiate regular communication with or send management reports to customer representatives.
- Irregular business reviews. More than three months have gone by without the VOP provider attempting to schedule a formal business review. (Six months would be the longest tolerable period, if everything is going smoothly.)
- High stress and anxiety. Less-than-optimal VOP programs typically are accompanied by a climate of discomfort and anxiety. Contingent workers and traditional workers feel uncomfortable and uncertain as to their status and the direction of the program.
- Unclear processes. When VOP program processes are unclear or unworkable, contingent workers don't know whom to contact with questions or in the event of a problem. They may approach the customer directly when the issue should be resolved with the VOP provider. Similarly, the customer may be uncertain as to whom to contact with any questions or problems. This includes supervisors, managers and human resource representatives at the customer site.
- No contact with sub-vendors. When a VOP program provider tries to cut off all communication between the customer and backup staffing suppliers, the VOP provider creates a climate of distrust.

- Poor representative-hiring manager communication. Poor communication between the on-site VOP manager and end-users at the customer site result in unexpected and unexplained gaps in contingent worker coverage. This may also occur due to a lack of proactive inquiry and planning by the VOP provider.
- Complaints. There may be "surprise" complaints by contingent workers to administrative agencies that should have been anticipated and avoided by the on-site VOP manager. Similarly, there may be "unnecessary" complaints to customer management that should have been anticipated and avoided by the on-site VOP manager.
- The rumor mill reigns. Rumors become the primary vehicle through which job-related information is disseminated to the contingent workforce.
- Gaps in coverage. Gaps in coverage occur because late or absent contingent workers are not immediately replaced by the on-site VOP manager.
- Low contingent productivity. The contingent workforce does not appear as productive as the traditional workforce, even after correcting for obvious differences in training and experience.
- Lack of confidence. The customer is not confident that the VOP provider really understands (or even cares about) its needs.

VOP programs with human resource management options

Most staffing firms have the capacity to provide an array of human resource management, as well as staffing services. The object of the exercise should be to determine how many current HR functions could realistically be turned over to the primary staffing vendor. Parenthetically, many organizations have been able to negotiate some of these HR services for their regular employees, as well as for the contingent workers, supplied by the staffing vendor.

Customers benefit by getting consistent treatment for their workers, but they must beware of the potential co-employment issues, which we address in chapter 6, "Mitigating Risk." They may also save money by shifting HR burdens to the staffing supplier. For example, testing and training are two obvious staffing elements that can be performed by either the staffing supplier or the customer organization.

If the staffing supplier has a credible testing, training, or performance evaluation program in place, it is to the customer's advantage to try to extend that program to all of its regular employees. Even if the number of contingent workers does not justify extending these services as a courtesy to all of an organization's employees, a small incremental fee can be negotiated to help offset the staffing firm's costs. More details on testing and training programs are discussed later in this chapter.

24/7 service options

VOP staffing is more than a 9-5 business. Typically, multiple-shift operations benefit from (but may not absolutely require) multiple shift coordinators. Some staffing firms respond to this challenge by having coordinators "straddle" two or three operating shifts. While this is not optimal for the customer, it may be workable, depending on the unique circumstances of the customer organization.

The VOP staffing configuration is very much subject to negotiation. Sometimes customer needs can be met with the efficient coverage strategy referred to above. But sometimes that efficiency results in a reduction in the level of service, or in the quality of the contingent workforce.

The first step is a realistic assessment of the feasibility of servicing multiple shifts, without continuous onsite coverage. The next step is to assess whether enlisting the support of the staffing firm's full-service branch network can substitute for continuous onsite coverage. The final step is to consider the feasibility of various options for being on-call, in which VOP coordinators have agreed to be accessible upon being texted or paged, within certain agreed upon parameters and response times. Staffing firms considering these options have to balance costs against the power of 24/7 service options to retain valued customers.

Ancillary service options

In a recent conversation, a senior purchasing officer of a Fortune 500 company commented that "if staffing firms bidding on our VOP are foolish enough to be willing to service our elevators as part of the agreement" he was going to "let them do it." It is a true story, albeit a bit over the edge of reasonableness. However, organizational customers may find themselves in the unusual circumstance of negotiating with staffing vendors who are looking for innovative opportunities to do more and more to initiate and cement a business relationship with potential customers.

Staffing firms have many core competencies and there is no reason that their VOP customers should not be able to avail themselves of these competencies, to their own advantage. Recruiting, testing, training and performance evaluation are obvious examples. The challenge is to determine which of the firm's competencies can actually add value to the customer's programs — at a reasonable price to the customer and reasonable margins to the staffing firm.

Backup recruitment options

Sometimes the recruiting needs of an organization can be fully met through on-site recruiting at the customer's facility alone. But often, effective recruiting must be augmented through the staffing supplier's branch network or through a remote recruiting facility set up by the VOP provider for that purpose. The customer is motivated to have a qualified workforce recruited on their behalf and available for assignment when needed. The staffing provider is similarly motivated to comply, but at the lowest cost and least disruption to their other operations and customers.

Staffing firms that cannot meet a customer's needs can extend their reach through developing a network of backup suppliers. Through such a network, staffing firms can provide service over a wider area or in niches that are not their specialty, and ultimately retain customers whose needs exceed the staffing firm's capability.

It is to the customer's advantage to understand exactly how the VOP provider will recruit on their behalf, so there will be no misunderstanding. Backup procedures should be agreed upon in advance. This is important even for large staffing suppliers, with a multitude of strategically located branch offices that should be able to support the VOP. It is even more critical for smaller suppliers that may have greater difficulty obtaining "internal" backup from their own, more limited, branch network.

The most effective solution usually lies in a reliable network of secondary or backup suppliers. This allows even the smallest staffing supplier to level the playing field in the VOP support arena. But the process is by no means automatic. It takes planning, organization and relationship building skills on behalf of the primary staffing supplier that is running the VOP. And it also takes good faith and fair dealing to make it work.

If a primary supplier is unwilling to relinquish orders until it is too late to fill them properly, or if it is unwilling to pass anything other than unfillable orders to backup suppliers, or if it attempts to steal contingent workers from its backup suppliers, then, not surprising, the best and most qualified backup suppliers will not be willing to work with that primary vendor. Primary suppliers that burn their bridges find that their service and the overall quality of the workers they can provide go downhill. This squeezes margins as the amount of work required to find acceptable workers increases. If quality dips too low, customers will back out of the VOP arrangement.

Competitive staffing firms know that the solution is to discuss remote recruiting, backup procedures and secondary supplier treatment in advance. Staffing firms must assure themselves that ethical business practices and fair treatment of backup suppliers are in place, as they are an essential component of the VOP program.

Business review and reporting options

As we addressed in chapter 2, we strongly advocate the utility of business reviews. There is no doubt as to their benefit for both staffing suppliers and customers. But it is useful to have an advance understanding of how frequently they will be conducted, and by whom, and which performance metrics will be included. Customers need to be confident that the staffing dimensions that will be measured and reported include those that are most meaningful to them.

For example, if assignment completion by contingent workers is especially important to the customer organization, perhaps because of orientation and adjustment issues, then the staffing firm should focus on the proportion of assignments completed in the review. Alternatively, if a customer is concerned about whether it is only being sent fully qualified workers for its openings, the staffing provider may wish to address the number of worker replacements that are required, the ratings that are given to the contingent workers by their supervisors within the customer organization, and the average scores on any skill testing devices that are used for worker selection and assignment.

There are similar performance metric options that may be specified for the ongoing performance reports that are produced, apart from the formal business reviews. There is great flexibility with respect to what is included within these reports, and how frequently they are produced. Beyond the standard metrics that a staffing firm regularly provides, customers may ask for additional metrics that they prefer.

Finally, the primary supplier should also report on the performance of the backup suppliers to the VOP program. Their performance continues to be the responsibility of the primary supplier. Savvy customers hold their VOP operators to the typical "industry standard" commitment to insure excellent service for their organization, regardless of who provides that service, be it the primary or the backup suppliers.

Provide Additional Human Resources Services

Competitive staffing firms provide additional human resources services in a strategic manner. Some of these services have become expected as tools to protect against hiring bad apples, keep contingent workers' skills up to date, or to promote better matches between contingent workers and customers' organizational cultures. In this section, we examine the value of providing training, testing and background checks and references. We also review some best practices in the design and evaluation of training, testing contingent workers, and using background checks and references.

Training

Delivering training to contingent staff can increase candidate quality in high-volume service lines and increase success rates in any line. The value of training and the measurement of training outcomes has increased. However, training improperly provided can create liability when it triggers co-employment issues. (See chapter 6 for a discussion of these issues.) There is no standard of care when it comes to training. Customers' expectations keep rising. But a smart staffing firm serving high-volume service lines can use training to differentiate itself. Here, we discuss when, what, how, and how not to provide training.

The value of training and measurement of outcomes has increased

Training of one kind or another has been part of the staffing industry almost since its beginnings in the 1940s. But its role has continued to expand until it has become almost ubiquitous within the last decade. Outside of the highly specialized service lines and niches, most staffing suppliers have incorporated more and more training opportunities into their recruiting and retention process.

The sophistication of the training has increased as well, with most staffing suppliers using computerized training that provides direct and immediate feedback to users. Often this is accomplished without the need for supplier staff even to be in the loop. Of course, they want to be involved just as soon as a certain level of proficiency is reached, in order to dispatch qualified workers before their competitive staffing suppliers gain an opportunity to do so. Measuring learning outcomes immediately enables staffing suppliers to know precisely when proficiency has been achieved and to document to customers that their contingent workers are up to par.

The increasingly common integration of testing and training into a single program module has facilitated and automated the recruiting, evaluation and dispatching process. In the last decade, staffing suppliers have become far more effective and efficient in turning applicants into revenue-generating workers on assignment. And the self-paced nature of the testing and training has made for a more positive user experience from the perspective of an applicant who has been recruited by the staffing supplier.

Increasingly, the staffing industry has begun to move toward remote testing and training for its applicants. Online testing and training programs have been increasing in sophistication and user-friendliness. Clearly, they are the wave of the future. We have only begun to experience the changes that they will continue to make within staffing operations. Of course there are many issues that have been problematic in their early introduction this past decade, such as protecting security (e.g., just who is it really taking the test remotely?), proprietary information and confidentiality. But these are in the process of getting resolved and they have not stopped the inexorable movement toward the extraordinary convenience of remotely administered testing and training.

Why the emphasis on training? Why not simply have selected qualified workers to begin with? There were a number of reasons:

- Many service lines suffer a painful lack of qualified workers, and traditional recruiting alone has not been able to meet demand. Training eager workers who have the right attitude and abilities but lack the complete requisite skill sets can be an effective solution.
- The "half-life" of job skills, especially technical job skills, is becoming shorter and shorter. Consequently, both workers and customers feel the need to continuously build new skills.
- Workers in the last decade have recognized that they were becoming commoditized and all that they had to sell in the market was their current skills. Thus they valued staffing suppliers (as well as employers) who helped them keep their skill sets fresh and up to date. Thus they were more likely to be loyal to firms that helped them maintain their marketability and that recognized and compensated them for their enhanced skills.
- The best workers in the marketplace were most likely to apply to staffing firms that had the reputation of a commitment to training and upgrading skills. Thus it became a self-fulfilling prophecy that suppliers that made the most visible effort to upgrade applicant skills also attracted the workers with the best skills and motivation to begin with. While some staffing firms still assume an elitist attitude and maintain that only the most qualified applicants seek them out for employment, they may end up driving away the best applicants by not providing training.
- Staffing suppliers learned that they could pay less for workers who had recently upgraded their skills, especially for workers who had upgraded their skills at the very same staffing firms that were then hiring them and dispatching them to their clients. This strategy was especially beneficial for suppliers that predominantly negotiated contracts that only specified bill rates and not pay rates. The increased gap between the two rates became pure profit!

What training to provide and when

Managers should be clear exactly what knowledge, skills and attitudes (KSAs) workers need to upgrade. They have a large set of choices as to what content to provide:

- Job-skills training boosts knowledge, skills, and attitudes needed for specialized, professional, or supervisory jobs. Because the content learned in these programs is so close to the actual behaviors performed on the job, these programs often have the most measurable impact on job performance. However, the more sophisticated knowledge and skills call for education and personal development rather than training. Staffing firms in specialized service lines with highly skilled workers and managers are less likely to provide this type of training.

- Workplace-related skills training boosts knowledge, skills, and attitudes in communicating with others, working in teams and with diverse people, and with all-purpose processes such as decision making and problem solving. Many of these programs involve not only boosting workers' skills, but also improving their attitudes. Courses required by law, such as sexual harassment training, are included in this category. New-hire orientation courses introduce people to the mission, vision, values, policies, and logistics for specific companies.

- Basic skills training boosts knowledge and skills to the level typically provided by elementary schools. This includes reading, writing, arithmetic, basic computer literacy and English language. Staffing firms that provide large numbers of low-wage workers can benefit from ensuring that their contingent workers can understand and follow instructions and have the prerequisite knowledge to learn how to use computerized equipment.

Smart staffing firms align the training that they provide with their customers' strategic and financial needs. Most of training programs are available in a generic form, and some can be customized to fit a specific company. Generic skills training is inexpensive because online training providers sell modules and charge low fees, on either a per-person or subscription basis.

Customized training is much more expensive because it must be redesigned repeatedly for each company. However, customized training can teach company-specific values and policies while teaching workplace or job-specific skills. To some companies, this is of great strategic importance. For instance, customer-service training at a company such as Nordstrom or Starbucks would be tailored to providing a very special level of customer service that turns the company's values into customer-friendly behaviors.

One form of customized training that makes a big difference in a contingent worker's early performance is job orientation. Staffing firms can fit job orientation into their procedures for dispatching contingent workers. VOP representatives can provide client-specific orientation using materials already in use by the client firm. Orientation can even prevent problems prior to dispatching when orientation shows a worker that they are not a good fit for the job.

From a human resource management perspective, we have learned that the probability of a contingent worker being successful on an assignment is often a function of how much they know about a position before they accept it and before they actually start work. Part of the reason is that an effectively conducted orientation program gives prospective workers the opportunity to deselect themselves if they do not perceive a good fit, from their perspective. In many ways, the workers' assessment of the quality of a match with the job may be more important than that of the actual customer — and more predictive of the successful completion of an assignment.

It is to the advantage of smart staffing suppliers to know as quickly as possible if a prospective worker is unlikely to be successful. This reduces their costs in that most firms provide performance guarantees that protect their customers but still require that they pay contingent workers whom they dispatch to a job site — typically for a minimum of four to eight hours. In addition, it protects their reputation, both with their customers and with their temporary workers, not to dispatch people in situations in which they are not likely to be successful or satisfied.

When should staffing firms provide training? They should provide training only under a few conditions:

- Training should be provided only for skills that can be learned during the span of a training program and those skills that fill the gap between workers' current skill set and the skills they will need on the job.

- They should provide training only to workers who are motivated and have the prerequisite skills. Workers with poor motivation to learn and weak job skills should be given a program or discussion that boosts their motivation or be dropped from the payroll.
- The development or purchase of a training program should cost far less than the likely benefit. Some practitioners have advocated using the classic return-on-investment approach to determine the utility of all training and selection programs. Historically, effective training programs have enjoyed an especially impressive rate of return.
- They should provide training at a time when workers will be using the skills immediately after and even during the training program. Jonathan worked for a company that provided excellent software training to a client. The client later complained that the training didn't work and demanded that $1 million be returned! A brief investigation found that workers received the training, passed assessments with flying colors, and thought they learned a lot. Unfortunately, the client hadn't installed the software until several weeks after the training program ended, and the workers forgot what they had learned.

There is one situation in which a staffing firm should offer training regardless of whether these criteria are met. When it costs nothing for the staffing firm to include additional applicants in a training program, smart staffing firms give an open invitation. It's a goodwill gesture that often builds workers' loyalty to the staffing firm. Anyone with the time, motivation, and opportunity to partake in training should be encouraged to do so.

The training design and evaluation process

Good training is targeted. The training profession has developed a system to discover the target and design, deliver, and evaluate training aimed at that target. Large staffing firms should have a training professional on staff who knows instructional systems design (ISD) and can use it to ensure that the training delivered is effective.

The first step is conducting a needs analysis. At this stage, training or human resources professionals determine the gaps between workers' current knowledge, skills, and attitudes (KSAs) and the levels needed to do the job well. They also estimate whether it's feasible to lift the current level high enough through affordable training.

A good needs analysis produces a clear list of learning objectives that describes the KSAs that workers will have at the end of training, a description of the constraints — such as cost, locations and available delivery methods — that a training program will have to meet, and a plan for how trainees will be assessed and the effectiveness of the training will be evaluated. When off-the-shelf training is available that meets these constraints, all that is required is assessing each worker for their personal KSA levels and to match those with existing training programs.

KSA Soup

Some people say that KSA stands for knowledge, skills, and abilities. That's fine for selection purposes, because you need to hire people with abilities that are prerequisite to a job. Some selection experts say that they look at a person's KSAOs or KSAPs, where O stands for "other attributes" and P stands for "personal qualities." However, by definition, training doesn't influence stable attributes like abilities and personal qualities. Education and experience influence some abilities over time, but training is too brief to do that. When talking about training, we should make KSA stand for the things that training can influence, which are knowledge, skills, and attitudes.

Smart staffing firms and smart customers make it easy for training and human resources professionals to gather the information needed to do a complete needs analysis. It is far cheaper to discover roadblocks to effective training during the needs analysis than to run into them in the middle of an expensive design process or after training has been delivered.

The next steps are designing the instruction, developing the materials, and implementing the training program. In the case of pre-designed training, this has already been done, and the only thing needed is to select the appropriate training modules.

The final step is training evaluation. Evaluation serves three major functions: to determine whether trainees have achieved the stated objectives of the training program, to provide feedback that can improve future programs training, and to help justify the costs of training programs. Evaluation can document the worth of training by indicating whether key business objectives were actually achieved and/or risky behavior diminished as a result of the training.

The levels of effectiveness

The earliest model for evaluating the effectiveness of training, still the basis for today's thinking, was introduced in 1959 by the psychologist D. L. Kirkpatrick. He described four levels of evaluation criteria.

Level 1, trainees' reaction, measures the trainee's impression of the program. Usually, these are measured with "smile sheets," called that because they often just measure the person's enjoyment of the training and satisfaction with the program. But recent research has shown that asking trainees about their intention to use what they learned in the training program correlates pretty well with actual use of that behavior back on the job.

Level 2, learning criteria, measures how much trainees have learned in the program. These criteria often are assessed through a written or computerized test that evaluates the knowledge acquired in the program that is necessary for effective performance in this aspect of the job. Computers these days can measure some actual behaviors, such as typing speed and accuracy and even correctness of pronunciation. When an important skill cannot be measured with a paper or computerized test, other, more expensive measures should be deployed.

Level 3 measures behaviors used on the job. Good evaluations measure the behaviors learned in training that are most directly related to success on the job. Supervisors or human resources professionals can observe on-the-job performance and rate workers' use of the specific behaviors taught in the training program. This is where the rubber meets the road.

Level 4, business results criteria, measures results that are affected by workers' behaviors targeted by the training program. These results could be productivity on the workers' jobs, customer satisfaction, sales or costs affected by those behaviors, or broader organizational outcomes and performance objectives. This level goes beyond the previous level to ask how effectively the training influences actual results.

Some experts suggest that the scope of training evaluation be expanded to include a fifth level, return on investment (ROI) criteria. This measure provides a way to determine the cost-effectiveness of training programs. For example, ROI would try to determine whether training produces enhanced job performance — or reduces the number of charges of discrimination, retaliation and harassment — to an extent greater than the cost of training itself.

Collectively, these five levels can be aggregated to assess the overall acceptance and effectiveness of a training program that develops job skills and supports risk management, and to determine the need for modification, expansion or repetition.

The key take-away is that staffing firm managers need to drive training evaluation. Without evaluation, training is pointless. There is no way to know whether it is effective without measuring its results. At the very least, staffing companies and employers need to assess the effectiveness and outcome of training programs as a defensive measure to protect against claims of negligence and abuse. (For that matter, regularly scheduled internal reviews can help to evaluate the effectiveness of all employment practices, not only training.) Once it is proven effective, the evaluation can be used as the basis for making decisions about the frequency, content, and methods for subsequent training.

Testing

Companies that don't select the best talent leave those people for the competition. Companies that do a poor job of fitting people to positions lower their customers' productivity and their contingent workers' satisfaction. Unstructured interviews are notoriously ineffective at selecting candidates. While structured interviews are more effective, they take a long time. To solve these problems, competitive staffing firms use employment tests to weed out weak candidates and to better match people to positions.

Most staffing firms now employ skills assessment and psychological testing programs in an effort to deliver better, more culturally compatible employees to their clients. Effective tests reduce subjectivity and human error in selection decisions in high-volume service lines. Some staffing firms have developed their own testing programs, while others use programs from one of the dozens of assessment tool vendors.

Benefits and types of assessments

Tests are useful for measuring knowledge, skills, attitudes, and abilities that can be assessed directly using pencil and paper or computers. No one wants to estimate word processing proficiency in an interview! But a computer can be used to do it.

Tests can be administered to a large number of people and scored quickly. The scores can be added to interview results to provide a more robust analysis of individuals' fit for a job. Tests require a lot less work than interviews when a large number of candidates must be reviewed for a small number of positions. This makes them ideal for use in high-volume service lines.

Although these testing programs may seem similar at first glance, some are much more likely than others to yield the quality results you're looking for. And some can even land a company in legal hot water. No one — not even the best experts — can read a test and know whether it works or not. Smart staffing firms use only tests that have undergone rigorous validation studies showing that they actually predict performance on the jobs for which candidates have applied.

Three of the most common types of tests are job sample tests, cognitive ability tests, and personality tests. Each has a different use in predicting job performance.

Testing a candidate's performance on sample job tasks is a direct way to predict their performance on the job. Such assessments measure candidates' performance time, quality, and quantity. Actors and singers engage in this process every time they audition. Staffing firms can give administrative assistants timed typing, spreadsheet, or filing tasks. Managers can be given simulated tasks, the most famous of which is called the "in-basket" task. In this assessment, a manager must prioritize a set of letters, memos, reports, and emails, and then plan the next few hours or days accordingly.

Cognitive ability correlates with performance on complex and knowledge-based jobs, so employers have turned increasingly to tests of cognitive ability. Some specialized cognitive ability tests predict performance on jobs that require those abilities. For instance, spatial relations tests help predict pilot ability to stay oriented in three-dimensional space. Clerical aptitude tests help predict performance on clerical jobs where accuracy and speed are important.

Personality tests measure such dimensions as extroversion, agreeableness, conscientiousness, openness, and emotional adjustment. These tests' results are made a bit less accurate by the fact that test takers are reporting on themselves. However, research has shown that some personality dimensions, as measured by self-reports, can still predict performance. For instance, extraversion and agreeableness predict sales and management performance. Conscientiousness predicts how hard people work across most jobs.

Validation is a must

For any test to be defensible in court, it must be validated. The tasks in a job sample test should match the tasks that the candidate will actually be given on the job. Describing job content is part of "job analysis." If the tasks match, then the test is said to have "content validity." With other sorts of tests, content validity is not defensible. Those tests must be demonstrated to predict actual performance on the target job. That is called "criterion-related validity."

Validation is expensive. So tests should be used for positions where their cost is warranted, such as when many candidates apply for a small number of positions. Managers can conduct a cost-benefit analysis to determine the practical value for using each validated test. We discuss how test validation works in chapter 6.

Background checks and references

Background checks and references help to avoid unreliable or dangerous workers. A full background check is more effective than the common reference check, but can add significantly to the initial cost of providing candidates. Full background checks can include degree verification, credit checks, drug screening, and criminal record searches. It is our opinion that over time, these background checks serve to reduce overall staffing costs.

Many customers expect that staffing firms screen and evaluate prospective workers for appropriate skills and check their backgrounds and references. The need to check a job applicant's references is obvious. Credible surveys suggest that as many as one-third of all applicants misrepresent some aspect of their backgrounds.

Most companies check references before hiring to fill white collar jobs. In fact, according to some estimates, more than 80 percent of all companies do so. But when it comes to applicants for blue-collar jobs, the number drops below 70 percent and to below 60 percent for part-time employees. Some sources suggest that when it comes to contingent workers, as few as two in five companies check references.

That's not good enough. Even if problems do not emerge, a less-than-thorough background check may leave a staffing company with a worker who delivers unfulfilled expectations and dissatisfaction rather than productivity and a job well done.

In some cases a background check will be a computerized search of criminal court records in the one or two counties nearest an applicant's current home or job. Other companies order a search in every county in which an applicant has lived or worked during the last five years. Some background checking companies even promote the fact that they actually send investigators to search court records in relevant counties, rather than simply relying on online searches. (These increased levels of background checking may add significantly to costs and result in higher bill rates for staffing services.). National background checks are extremely expensive and time consuming and typically not done for most employment situations.

A staffing firm best practice involves tracking candidates' career movements through systematic and comprehensive reference checks to guide a background check rather than relying simply on candidates' self-reports of where they lived and worked.

Effective background checks should not be limited to criminal matters. Credit checks, verification of academic degrees and drug screening are playing an increasing role in insuring that there will be no unpleasant surprises after a worker is hired.

The nature of a reference check varies widely in the staffing industry as well. For some staffing suppliers, a reference check can consist of as few as two attempted calls to references that the applicant suggests. Others require that there be one or two completed calls. Still others require that calls be completed to at least two of an applicant's recent employers.

Some staffing companies will be satisfied to take "no" for an answer (as in, "We only confirm titles and dates of employment"), while others train their staffers to probe for more. Some even request help from the applicants in inducing former employers to share more information about their job performance.

To make all this checking as efficient as possible, staffing firms would be well-advised to have all applicants sign a release that permits credit checks and allows former employers to be contacted for references and waives any legal right to sue anyone who supplies the requested information.

The bottom line is that reference and background checks can be done in a cost-effective manner. They protect a staffing firm and its customers' interests and are expected by most customers.

Structure the Staffing Firm to Provide Effective Services

Deciding what services to provide is one thing. Building an operation that provides those services efficiently and effectively is another. Basically, staffing firms do two things: get customers and provide the services that retain them. We now discuss how to structure the sales and service operations in a staffing firm so each does a good job.

Keep sales and service separate

The most successful staffing managers focus on metrics. They call on their staff to produce results and measure those results. Managers don't ask staff to do two potentially competing priorities at once because they know that this will only diminish both. Yet, many companies do just that. They succumb to the allure of the everyone-sells approach.

It is not that companies don't benefit from the incremental effort of every employee taking a customer-oriented approach to all transactions. They do. Rather, the problem is the unintended consequences of making everyone accountable for everything, which effectively makes no one accountable for anything. This is not an overstatement; it's the harsh reality of people in organizations.

Why managers put sales and service together

The principles of responsibility and accountability are not new. So why do so many staffing firms try to integrate sales, service, and often even customer retention? The answers are as seductive as they are unfortunate:

1. Staffing firms, often desperate for sales, feel the need to do something — anything — different. Companies feel pressure to change in the *worst* way, and that is *exactly* what they do!

2. Management consultants, ourselves included, often tout the need for everyone to take responsibility for the success of their company. This is often misconstrued as requiring that all employees become part of the sales process, regardless of fit or logic.

3. Increased scrutiny of every element of company overhead has led managers to redesignate service and operations staff into a more defensible and less vulnerable quasi-sales capacity. This is a transparent disguise that will cost, rather than save, scarce resources.

4. The traditional friendly rivalry between sales and service (i.e., "sales doesn't work hard, makes too much money, and gets to shop and have great lunches out" while "service gets to relax in the office, has no responsibility for building the business and is never blamed for not making budget") has encouraged management to try to build cohesiveness by marrying these responsibilities. This strategy is counterproductive and only serves to *exacerbate* turf issues.

5. "Shared responsibility" has a very pleasing and egalitarian flavor that makes it easy to present and hard to dismiss. Unfortunately, it doesn't work.

Why doesn't it work? Because people can only really focus on one thing at a time. And when sales and service call for different behaviors to achieve its goal, workers must choose only one of those behaviors. Would you combine sales and manufacturing in the automobile industry? How about combining sales and operations in the shipping industry? Of course not.

So why try it in the staffing industry? Even though people are a different kind of product from Buicks, it still makes no sense.

Not that it isn't a good exercise to let all staff briefly experience all positions as part of their orientation or development. It is also reasonable for all employees to pitch in and help during temporary overloads. But build it in structurally? Absolutely not.

The most important reason to avoid combining responsibility for sales, service, and customer retention is to be able to apply metrics and ensure accountability for *each* of these critical functions. This cannot be accomplished reliably when responsibilities overlap. And without accountability, we know that performance is unlikely to improve on its own.

The bottom line is that, while senior managers must inevitably be held accountable for the success of their entire operation, they must segregate responsibilities below them to gain control over performance. With similar logic, the higher the reporting relationships that management can affect for sales, service, and customer retention on an individual basis, the higher the probability that someone with the authority to influence a positive outcome will actually do so.

Individual accountability works best

Many decades of research and observation have documented the fact that employees focus on what is measured and reported. This concept is not difficult to understand. But managers assume that you can add responsibility for multiple functions (i.e., sales, service, and customer retention) as long as you have some way to measure each incremental function. This is partly true, but it misses the point.

The point is well known and understood by marketing professionals and advertising agencies. They recognize that to be effective, an advertisement should have only one theme because the audience can't focus on more than one thing at a time. Neither can most workers.

Moreover, the process of expanding accountability typically causes performance degradation in the employees' area of primary responsibility. It also creates a ready excuse for performance deficiencies and a lack of focus. Not surprisingly, weaker employees typically love it because diffused responsibility allows them to focus on what they enjoy doing or what is easiest, not on what you really need them to do. Expanding accountability so that it is shared creates pseudo-accountability and destroys true accountability.

Employees should be held accountable only for what they were hired to do and rewarded for what they accomplish. This management approach works with almost everybody all of the time. It doesn't mean that everyone will always be successful, but it does mean that ineffective performers will rarely escape detection and that you will have an opportunity to counsel and coach them, if appropriate.

You have tried integration and you think it works

Not likely. It's more likely that the overall business environment (inside and outside your firm) was responsible for the "success" and that the integration of sales, service, and customer retention functions made little difference.

If you integrated those functions recently, it is probable that the destructive impact of your well-intentioned job expansion has not yet become manifest in diminished performance. Be patient. After the novelty and excitement wear off, employees tend to revert to the task they find most enjoyable or in which they are most effective.

Managers should avoid assessing the efficacy of integration based on initial employee reactions. Employees usually show enthusiasm at first, when everything seems possible. Then, reality hits and "slippage" begins to occur in at least one of the three areas. Your best and most productive employees will tend to notice the problem first — typically as their performance-based incentive compensation begins to slide.

In our experience, there is no generic pattern to this performance-related slippage. It is literally a function of employees' work propensity and skill sets, coupled with a random factor associated with whichever function breaks down first: sales, service, or customer retention.

If you are beginning to conclude that this is no way to run a company, you are correct.

Are there exceptions?

Of course there are. Very small companies may have no choice — at first. For example, a start-up branch may not have the staffing configuration to do it right. But all it takes is two people to start — the traditional "one for sales and the other for service," because customer retention is not yet a pressing issue.

Very large companies (nationals and multinationals) have complex organizational structures and a great deal of inertia when it comes to change. They also tend to do what they do for reasons that may not be apparent — or even logical — from a business perspective. It may take them years to detect structural errors, and even then they may not have the incentive or the will to diagnose them and institute changes. (The classic ocean liner paradigm comes to mind. Steering and speed adjustments to a giant ship do not become manifest for many miles.)

Significantly understaffed companies' resources may be inadequate to segregate sales, service, and customer retention effectively throughout their operations. This is not a desirable state of affairs and should not be interpreted as healthy management frugality that can be sustained over time.

Improperly staffed companies may not have the caliber of employees needed to perform each function. As a result, they find it necessary to "stretch" their more competent and capable employees over a variety of positions to compensate for the inadequacy of employees with primary responsibility for functions that they are not able to handle without support. Again, this is not a sustainable situation for a competitive company.

The bottom line

The most competitive companies continue to separate sales, service, and customer retention responsibilities, and maintain that separation as high as possible in their organizations. They do not succumb to the ephemeral allure of integrating these functions to "achieve internal staffing efficiencies" or accommodate employee preferences. Effective management requires specific accountability, quantifiable performance metrics, and focused attention by individuals who accept responsibility for discrete operational outcomes. Anything less results in long-term, sub-par performance and unnecessarily missed opportunities for excellence.

Chapter Four

MARKETING AND BRANDING THE COMPANY AND ITS SERVICES

Staffing firms come in a variety of flavors. Some are like high-volume restaurants while others are like gourmet bistros. Highly competitive staffing firms set their strategy to match their customers' needs and select their customers to match their strengths so that they can execute their strategies well. A high-volume customer requires a high-volume staffing firm, while a customer needing hard-to-find specialists requires a bistro.

Customers differ in their service-line characteristics, mode of operations, and geography. For instance, one customer may be a national company that hires large numbers of temporary accountants on short notice for brief, countrywide audits. Another customer may be a local company that tends to hire a steady stream of administrative temps over a long period and can predict well ahead of time when those positions will open. Staffing firms must serve these two customers differently.

Most often, staffing firms adjust how they serve their customers by matching their customers' service line needs for speed, quality, price, and customer service. Competitive staffing firms usually develop one or two of these as an area of strength where they can out-compete their rivals.

But setting strategy is not enough. Staffing firms must also execute well. This provides significant challenges — especially when execution requires organizational change. For instance, a staffing supplier must operate differently in order to serve the sudden needs of the accounting audit customer than it would to serve the customer needing a steady supply of administrative assistants. Similarly, a staffing firm must change its operations in order to shift from providing high-quality service to high speed or to shift from local to national customers. Highly competitive staffing firms assess whether such a change is worth it. They can assess their readiness for such a change and estimate the costs of change. The challenge of execution and the cost of change are the reasons why staffing firms can usually compete on one or two areas of strength, but not usually all four at once. The best staffing firms know where to focus.

Service Line Characteristics Shape Staffing Firm Strategy

As we mentioned earlier, staffing firms must serve different customers differently. But it's the characteristics of service lines themselves that most influence what strategy staffing firms must adopt. For instance, a single customer may ask for a large number of contingent office-clerical staff and also a few specialized accountants. The staffing firm must serve those service lines a bit differently. The characteristics that matter most are the level of contingent worker volume, the balance of open positions versus candidates in the overall labor market, and how mature the service line is.

Service lines like office-clerical staff and light industrial workers are usually high volume. The American Staffing Association reported in 2005 that 62% of Fortune 500 companies hire office-clerical contingent workers from staffing firms and 58% hire light industrial contingent workers. Companies often use contingent workers in such high-volume service lines to ramp up new projects. The faster they do so, the quicker they can get new products to market. High volume service lines require that staffing firms have a pool of available candidates that they can provide on short notice.

Low-volume service lines, such as legal or sales and marketing staff, call for a similar strategy, but the costs to the staffing firm are higher on a per-worker basis. Because the internal costs cannot be made up for in volume, they must be incorporated into the markup. Training and orientation of contingent workers becomes more specialized and thus more difficult to incorporate as a courtesy in order to solicit new business. Staffing firms can offer such training and orientation as an add-on service for additional fees. Staffing firms usually assign their more sophisticated employees to service the needs of specialized, low-volume contingent workers and customers.

Cutting-edge service lines require different strategies than mature service lines. In cutting-edge service lines, candidates may be hard to find, candidate quality may be difficult to define and measure. Such service lines may be costly to run and job openings may take time to fill, but if competitors are facing the same difficulties and customers' needs are strong, bill rates can be set high enough to provide generous profit margins.

Traditional staffing procedures may not work as well in a cutting-edge service line. Staffing firm managers and employees have had to come up with creative solutions. Flexible employees who love challenges, creativity, and problem solving become the high performers in cutting-edge service lines. These employees and situations call for managers to give their staff a different level of supervision and training than is required for more mature service lines where operations are better defined.

Cutting-Edge Services: Move Fast or Eat Dust

Back when nursing was cutting-edge, first-mover advantage was very important. Some early operators made a fortune by getting bought out by one or two national conglomerates that specialized in nursing. These conglomerates recognized early that this would be a high-demand niche and went after investor dollars to make acquisitions.

They persuaded investors that they had the management skills to identify, acquire, and integrate small operators and that building from scratch would take too much time. They knew that competition would grow rapidly until someone developed a dominant national brand in nursing. By buying small operators that had learned the business, they were able to get a two- to three-year head start on potential competitors that had not yet jumped into the market or did not have the resources to build a national brand.

Within a few years, each bought up small operators around the country and formed a national firm that got so entrenched that they became the go-to player. Small operators quickly learned to come to the conglomerates to sell their firms. The conglomerates did a good job of vetting potential acquisition candidates and steered clear of the "losers."

Similar to the stock market, when everyone has figured out that something is the "next big thing," it's time to move on. When your barber is recommending a hot oil company or real-estate buy, it's probably time to get out. In the staffing industry, when it became apparent to the least sophisticated operators that nursing and healthcare was where everyone needed to be, it no longer was. When speakers at staffing industry conferences began hearing questions about whether it was too late to enter that service line — it was! Consultants were still able to make money coaching their clients about how to start a nursing or health care service line. But beyond a certain point in time, new operations were not viable, except in a few untapped markets.

So the companies that succeeded in nursing were those that moved quickly. They either built from scratch and sold out or they judiciously but quickly acquired small operations to build a national presence before anyone else did.

Mature service lines are more automated, with standardized processes. There is less need for innovative training and more need for basic skills training and staff supervision to ensure that employees follow the standardized processes. Employees who love structure, routine, and efficiency become the high performers in mature service lines. Profit margins drop as service lines mature. So, speed and operational efficiency are hallmarks of highly competitive staffing firms that serve mature service lines.

When the balance of candidates and open positions leans toward a large number of available candidates, highly competitive staffing firms can compete by finding the top quality people. They can do well in this area by implementing more testing programs, providing superior orientation and training, and speeding up the dispatching of contingent workers. And superior customer service and responsiveness always creates a competitive advantage. Efficient staffing suppliers take advantage of the oversupply of workers to reduce pay rates and thus increase their profit margins or decrease the bill rate — or sometimes a bit of both.

When customers have too many positions chasing too few candidates, the best staffing firms develop referral programs, adjust their pay rates upward to draw good candidates from competitors, and provide training to candidates whose skills can be brought up to standard without too much effort by the staffing company or compromise by the customer. Most companies create referral programs. However, few pay a large enough referral incentive to get much juice from them. Similarly, most companies do not adjust pay rates quickly in response to changing market conditions. Most staffing firms fail to use training as a competitive weapon. Sometimes, they provide training without having assignments available quickly enough; they lose these candidates to their competitors who have assignments ready for them. Other companies don't check candidates' progress in training often enough to know when they are ready for assignments that require the new skills. Staffing firms that develop a reputation for treating candidates well are more likely to succeed in attracting good candidates in a competitive economic environment.

Strategic Innovations Lead to Increased Profits ... for a Limited Time

When staffing firms see opportunities to better meet their customers' business strategy, customers are often willing to pay more. These opportunities usually show up as new services or new levels of candidate or service quality. When a customer's strategy relies on speed, the staffing firm's innovation may need to be one of speed. For instance, in fast-changing industries, companies that are first-to-market with cutting-edge products get huge, first-mover advantage. These customers need to be served by staffing firms that can help them staff projects very quickly.

Quick response requires pre-screening applicants in order to have a deep bench. The downside is having contingent workers wait around for assignments. Competitors may pick them up. Cutting-edge staffing firms solve this problem by paying contingent workers to be on standby. This is only viable for highly profitable service lines in highly competitive environments.

Once, computerized prescreening was cutting-edge. It was expensive and only open-minded early adopters risked using it. They figured out how to make it work. Today, such software is relatively inexpensive. And almost all staffing firms now use increasingly sophisticated matching software. However, to make standby pay profitable, staffing firms must conduct a financial analysis so as not to bleed cash.

Staffing firms can also innovate in operations to increase speed of dispatch and volume of contingent workers while decreasing costs per contingent worker at the same time. For instance, when software takes over transactions that once required human activity, a staffing firm can do them more quickly, at a lower cost, and for a larger number of contingent workers at a time. When software innovations also enable increases in candidate quality, firms may be able to increase speed, quality, and bill rate simultaneously.

In the early days of information technology, companies that implemented computerized skills testing and certification software had an immediate advantage over companies that simply screened education and prior job experience — and estimated skill-level from that limited information. Computerized testing saved labor, money, assessed candidates more rapidly, and ensured a consistently higher caliber of dispatches. Over time, that translated into the ability to obtain higher bill rates.

We can imagine what some innovations might look like over the next few years. By the time this book is in print, some of these may have come to pass or been taken over by unexpected changes. With cell phones with Internet access becoming more prevalent, cutting-edge staffing firms will find innovative ways to send candidates increasingly customized alerts for jobs with desired characteristics in desired locations, enabling them to respond immediately by texting, calling, or emailing.

Similarly, Web-based polling has become cheap, enabling companies to use pulse polls to keep in touch with workers on specific topics of current interest. These can be used to get instant feedback from contingent workers in high-volume positions. They could also be used to get feedback from customers on the performance of each contingent worker. If such data are gathered well, it could help identify high-quality contingent workers so that they get the best placements when their current engagement is complete.

Web 2.0 and its successors will be used creatively to reach out to potential new recruits, stay connected with contingent workers, link primary and backup suppliers, and keep customers in the loop. Further down the line, innovations that are now immature and not used at all in staffing will become useful to imaginative staffing firm executives. Take collaborative filtering — a technology used by music Web sites to mine millions of songs and millions of people's differing taste in music to help people find music that lights their fire. It is supposed to build communities of interest on the Web and help rate levels of quality. It does help build community, but it mostly determines what is popular. If Web community technologists get it right, collaborative filtering or a close cousin may end up helping make matches between people and the music that is a match to their taste. It is only one step further to develop a system that matches people and the jobs that are a match for their skills and taste in work.

Using an Innovation to Build a Moat around the Firm

As we saw in the previous section, some people made a killing by aggregating or being bought out in a rapidly growing market. Others made a killing by finding a profitable solution to a tough problem — a solution that was difficult for new entrants to replicate.

When it became apparent that there was a dearth of skilled nursing talent available to staffing companies in many markets, some proactive and creative operators found new solutions. Some sent recruiters to foreign countries and others negotiated with recruiters in those countries. They offered signing bonuses and relocation packages. The pay differential was so great that they were able to quickly recoup their investment by paying foreign nurses much less than they would have had to pay American nurses to lure them from their attractive positions. Successful operators had the sophistication to understand international regulations related to this practice.

Still other operators elected to move nursing talent temporarily around the country to best respond to local marketplace demand. They developed an expertise in temporary relocation and temporary housing — an expertise that was not easily replicated by new operators. This served as a significant barrier to entry. The allure of free travel, free housing, and high pay attracted contingent nurses. Of course, not every market was equally attractive. That had to be dealt with by higher pay rates.

Everyone will use technological innovations, but not everyone will use them well. Many firms have implemented social networking systems only to find them go dark after creating initial buzz or being superseded by the next hot technology. Information technology suffers from the "garbage-in/garbage-out" syndrome. Survey technology is so easy to use that some large companies have flooded their workers and managers with pulse polls and longer surveys. And some people complain that business networking sites are already clogged with too many recruiters' announcements. Highly competitive staffing firms will prioritize the information they need to gather and ask only for information that will have an impact on decisions.

Customer service innovations

Some innovations involve improvements in customer service. That means increased responsiveness (returning calls quickly), acknowledging orders immediately, and providing status updates to customers as frequently as they want them. Being proactive — anticipating needs based on prior usage and having candidates available to fill those needs — is a form of customer service that also builds speed. Competitive staffing firms make courtesy calls to good customers and present high caliber candidates even when customers haven't asked for them. They may call such candidates "most placeable applicants" or "most placeable candidates." They also use these calls as a sales technique to entice potential customers.

As contingent staffing has moved to being a central tool for customers, good customer service has become an increasing priority. Good customer service can win over customers in a competitive market. It can also salvage a situation where the staffing firm sent in a bad candidate. It increases the communication of valuable business intelligence between customer and staffing firm and builds a bond that competitors find more difficult to penetrate.

But there is a catch. Good customer service is difficult in a high-volume business. And much of the staffing industry is high-volume. Typically, staffing firms must run mean and lean. As such, it takes special training and extraordinary effort to take advantage of all of the customer service opportunities. Managers can increase the likelihood that their employees engage in good customer service behaviors by putting metrics in place to measure them, by providing customer service training to build employees' skills at those behaviors, and by including customer service in regular supervision, such as regularly discussing employees' customer service metrics.

How important are customer service innovations?

Customers have more staffing options today than ever before and they are increasingly likely to exercise their options. While good customer service has always been taught and advocated by staffing firm owners and managers, 10 years ago customers were more tolerant of service lapses than they have become today. This is a function of a number of factors including an increasing reliance on contingent workers by many customers and a concomitant increasing expectation of a reliable "just-in-time" supply of these workers as they are needed.

This trend is not surprising in that many more customers have built contingent workers into their overall staffing strategy and structure during this past decade. Thus they have been forced to impose more stringent requirements on the staffing process in order to avoid potentially debilitating disappointments and failures. When contingent staffing was only used peripherally by most customers, and for vacation and illness relief, they were more tolerant of service lapses and disappointments. And as the better staffing suppliers exposed staffing customers to superior service practices over the years, they became more reliant on these practices and less tolerant of inferior performance.

Staffing failures and service lapses have become more visible throughout most organizations that are increasing their contingent worker usage and their operational centrality. Thus, it is more difficult to conceal staffing problems from the attention of higher decision makers within these organizations. The political risk of staffing service failure has become the catalyst for improved customer service demands in many instances.

Purchasing managers have also been responsible for improved customer service within the staffing industry by demanding it, often as part of the contractual commitment. The shift of staffing supplier selection responsibility from human resources to purchasing has facilitated the introduction and imposition of improved quality standards of operation. Apparently, purchasing managers have been less reluctant than HR managers to tell staffing suppliers how they are expected to behave and perform. And all the while, they demand better pricing as part of the bargain. No wonder many staffing suppliers are not enamored of purchasing managers!

Innovate again and again

Unfortunately for innovators, today's differentiator often becomes tomorrow's commodity. Highly competitive staffing firms differentiate themselves by providing services, or a level of quality, speed, or price, that other firms cannot copy. In time, however, other staffing firms learn to match the new service or the new level of quality, speed or price. Innovators must recognize when to innovate again in order to stay profitably ahead.

For instance, innovations developed by a software vendor or disseminated as best-practice by a consulting firm spread as quickly as staffing firms will buy the innovation or pay for the consulting firm's intervention. For example, vendor-on-premises (VOP) programs originated by creative staffing firms were enormously successful. Consulting firms shared this profitable practice, building staffing firms' capacity through sharing the concept, providing training, and setting up the software necessary to make VOP operational. VOPs spread rapidly in major markets and ultimately changed the face of the industry over a 10-year period.

Over those 10 years, the industry bifurcated into firms that utilize intellectual capital and those that do not. Firms that effectively utilize their intellectual and financial capital have been able to work smarter, not harder. Firms that have fallen into the "mass production" of interchangeable workers have generally remained profitable, but not consistently. And they have had to work harder. Their market value has diminished and staff turnover has been high, as it has become harder to keep up with those who work smarter. But other than that, commodity staffing is a great business!

We have moved into a phase of the staffing industry business cycle in which almost anyone can gain entry and play the game. Whether by franchise or by sheer entrepreneurial initiative, the number of individuals seeking to enter the staffing industry keeps rising. So has the number of quiet failures and disappearances.

Reviewing dozens of staffing industry business plans and funding proposals has revealed a general lack of reality testing and competitive intelligence that has become part of these plans. This helps account for the influx of unqualified operators who have underestimated the intellectual and financial capital required to run a competitive staffing business. Absent the ability to finesse the intricacies of operations necessary to compete effectively in an increasingly sophisticated staffing environment, it was inevitable that marginal players felt it necessary to compete predominantly on price. That created a race to the bottom.

On the positive side, firms that have gotten the message, and that have the requisite intellectual capital, have learned to use it to their competitive advantage, and to charge appropriately for their specialized knowledge and skill. Many customers — including most of the best ones — care more about quality and service than they do about price. Recruiters who grasp the true art of their profession, which transcends simply posting jobs on Monster, add real value and have real value within the staffing process. Within the last decade, customers have become increasingly perceptive and knowledgeable about best recruiting and staffing practices and more willing to pay for them.

Match capabilities to market needs

The unique capabilities that a company brings may not match the services that the market demands, especially after changes in the market or when a company considers expanding into new markets.

Staffing firms face a dilemma: how much to build their business around their capabilities vs. being market-driven. If the market changes, trying to add new capabilities to meet market demand might be too challenging to execute profitably. However, not going where the market goes may result in a decrease in business. The best companies figure out how to meld both their competencies and the demands of the market. In his insightful and influential book, *Good to Great*, Jim Collins reviewed empirical evidence and found that the most consistently profitable companies are those that do what they do better than anyone else, do what they are deeply passionate about (including their core values and purpose), and do what customers will pay for.

A company that matches its brand to its capabilities can deliver on its promises. When potential customers understand a staffing firm's brand, the right customers are attracted to having that firm supply their staffing needs.

Some staffing firms can use a well-recognized brand image and their internal capabilities that back up that image to extend themselves into new service lines. Robert Half had a high-quality image, attracted high-caliber candidates in accounting and finance, and so was able to demand higher margins than its competitors. It extended this to other service lines, going from a specialty brand to a general brand — which is opposite to the way the industry usually operates. By 2006, Robert Half provided staffing for finance and accounting, management of finance and accounting, administrative support, information technology, legal, creative, and auditing/risk consulting services.

A company that matches its brand to the market increases the size of the potential customer pool. When markets change, staffing firms have to consider changing their brand offerings in order to keep market share.

For example, staffing firms that found a huge market demand for nurses in locations different from where the nurses lived discovered that they had to grow relocation and temporary housing operations to get the nurses to where the market demand was. Another example has been staffing firms shifting to a vendor-on-premises business model because customers began to expect it.

How innovation starts and matures

How do process innovations get developed and disseminated? And how do innovators overcome obstacles to implementing those developments?

In some cases, managers or sharp employees inside the company come up with bright ideas. Top managers can encourage open discussion to increase the flow of such ideas. (See chapter 1 for more on this.)

Vendor-on-premises (VOP) programs are an example of an innovation developed from the inside. Developers of early VOP programs saw a gap in the market. They saw difficulties in communicating with customers. Their relationship with their contact people at the customer firm was fine. But their relationships with end users — hiring managers who supervise contingent workers — were too shallow to protect the relationship. Problems emerged that could not be responded to as readily from a branch office as they could on-site.

They also saw an opportunity. No one was actually providing services on site with a customer, where they could meet customer's needs more quickly and effectively. They also saw a way to integrate themselves within the customer system so that the competitors would have a tough time removing them from the customer.

The key to spreading VOP programs was to find customers who were willing to try out the experiment and employees who were good at building relationships. Early adopters found that VOP programs provided several benefits. Staffing firm managers saw that the overhead and lower bill rates were more than compensated for by deeper relationships with customers that increased customer retention and the share of the total contingent business at each customer company. They also uncovered business intelligence that lowered costs by preventing errors or enabling quick recovery when they happened. Many staffing firm employees who were assigned on-site duties enjoyed developing deeper relationships with customers. Customers liked the increased responsiveness, customer service, and contingent worker quality that came with well-run VOP programs. They also liked having the primary supplier do all of the coordination with the backup suppliers. After a couple of years, VOP had proven its value.

This new practice was disseminated in several ways. Some of the people who developed VOP programs were hired by other staffing firms, spreading the practice. Speakers spread success stories at the prestigious, annual Staffing Industry Executive Forum produced by Staffing Industry Analysts. Consultants brought it as a best practice to be picked up by other firms. Soon, customers began demanding it because they heard about the benefits of VOP programs from their colleagues. For instance, the purchasing managers at customers' firms saw the cost savings utility.

Like any innovation that calls for changes in behavior and mindset, VOP programs were greeted with skepticism by many. Many staffing firm managers balked at the extra overhead and apparent decreases in bill rates. They worried whether their firms could pull off this newfangled process and wondered whether it was worth investing in something that might just be a passing fad. Employees were concerned because VOP programs called for them to do work that was traditionally done by HR staff at customer companies. Staffing firm employees worried whether the HR staff would feel threatened and not only nix the VOP contract, but also terminate the relationship with the staffing supplier.

VOP programs threw another challenge at staffing firm managers. Staffing firms found that they needed to rely on competitors to fill some of the customer's contingent worker requirements. This called for strong relationship-building skills, especially diplomacy. In order to fill all of a customer's orders, VOP staffing suppliers had to develop a strong level of trust in competitors who acted as backup suppliers and with customers who had to count on the VOP staffing supplier to develop trusting relationships with the backup suppliers that were needed to deliver high-quality contingent workers quickly, despite their being competitors in other situations. We discuss this issue further in chapter 5.

VOP at maturity

Surveys conducted by Staffing Industry Analysts have shown that VOPs have rapidly gained momentum and become ubiquitous in large customer organizations. Those that implemented VOP programs well have profited and made life difficult for staffing firms that had to compete against them.

Some customers complain, not surprisingly, that many of the less-qualified operators have jumped on the VOP bandwagon, either out of necessity or simply not to miss out on a good opportunity after having lost their control to the more experienced staffing firms.

The big firms have continued to grow bigger and the rich firms to grow richer, but not as rapidly as before. There are many exceptions. Smaller staffing vendors that had established relationships with larger customers tended to hold onto those relationships despite strong competitive pressure from other suppliers. Although they often have had to make certain concessions in the process, typically involving pricing.

The exception to the exception is when competitors were able to secure a national contract and local staffing vendors only had a relationship with the local facility and did not have the resources or the ambition to attempt to service their customer in distant locations. While some vendors were able to negotiate an exception for a while, over the past decade most of the business reverted to the supplier under national contract, often with litigation or the threat of litigation, when large numbers of workers were "transitioned" from the original supplier to the new national supplier.

The smartest VOP suppliers expended considerable effort in order to lock themselves into their customers' front- and back-office operating systems. This made it increasingly costly and disruptive for customers to extricate themselves from their suppliers' VOP programs. And it was usually done with "malice and forethought." (We are not really criticizing the practice, as Jay has frequently coached clients as to how to best accomplish it!) Vendor management systems might have provided an alternative for some customers, but they have been disappointing in many respects and failed to gain substantial traction as an alternative to VOP in the staffing marketplace.

Vendor-driven technology innovation

VOP programs represented an innovation inspired from inside staffing firms. In other cases, consulting firms and software vendors could see possibilities that weren't visible to insiders who were too close to the daily details to see the whole picture. Online testing and interactive online training were promoted by vendors. Initially, staffing firms used traditional paper and pencil tests, especially in technical and clerical areas. For clerical workers, they also used timed performance tests on adding machines and typewriters. Some progressive staffing firms established their own customized paper and pencil tests, while others purchased tests from commercial vendors.

The advent of computers within the staffing industry allowed the testing process to be automated. Both pencil and paper tests and typing tests could be delivered more efficiently and scored more accurately by a computer, sometimes with instant feedback to the applicant. Proactive staffing firms adopted these practices to their competitive advantage. In the first year or two, those firms could evaluate candidates a bit faster and with less labor required; most of all, it was a cool sales feature that lent itself well to customer demonstrations. Before computerized testing became standard, customers viewed early adopters as cooler, more savvy and efficient. Whether or not we believe it to be true, some sales representatives persuaded customers that their technological sophistication translated into superior candidates.

Jay's Cutting-Edge Payoff

One day, in 1994, I bought a laptop for about $15,000 in today's money, a price that would cause my boss' jaw to drop. I asked our company's IT manager to create an animated demo that would show customers what computerized testing and candidate evaluation could accomplish. I walked into the swank offices of a large Los Angeles company headquarters with the only laptop in the area. The HR director's jaw dropped as I started up this cutting-edge device that did not even need to plug into the wall. He proceeded to enjoy a cup of coffee while the demo transfixed his attention. The resulting multi-million-dollar contract made it easy to seek reimbursement for the laptop. The computerized testing and resultant high-quality candidates allowed us to sustain this relationship for many years.

The advent of the Web enabled this process to go online. This allowed for instant updating of tests to reflect newly demanded skill sets. Before the dot-com crash, early adopters got the opportunity to show their connection to what was an exciting development that seemed to know no bounds.

Computer-based training went through a similar sequence, but took longer to mature. In the early days, computers had monochrome screens. Imagine a computer world without video. The programs were text-based and boring. Nevertheless, staffing firms' sales teams could wow customers with demos dressed up to evoke the sense of technology that had arrived, even though it didn't yet live up to its promise. With graphics and video, computer-based training began to take the place of live training. It could be delivered at any time and automatically tailored itself to each applicant's needs.

Computer-based training enabled staffing firms to retain the best workers, people who wanted to keep their skill sets fresh. Those workers were grateful to the staffing company for having provided the training and often went on challenging assignments at lower-than-market rates. This increased the margins of the staffing suppliers, who could charge higher bill rates, while customers received a wider selection of qualified workers.

Job preview videos allowed applicants to click on the faces of people they wanted to hear from and learn about the jobs for which they were applying. Applicants deselected themselves when they learned about job requirements that were not a good fit, improving the match between people and jobs. As with every other advance, early adopters were often able to wow their customers and improve the retention and completion rates of their placements — both key factors in customer satisfaction.

Growth Brings Change

Some of the greatest challenges arise when staffing firms branch out in scope. For instance, local staffing firms hold their own against national firms because they excel at serving the quirks of the local market. National firms derive a competitive advantage from their perceived ability to deliver reliably on performance satisfaction promises for nationwide or international assignments. Such promises tend to make service look similar from one branch to another, making it more difficult to serve quirks in the local market.

They also benefit from the financial cushion created by deep pockets; this cushion helps larger staffing firms recover from management mistakes that can sink a smaller staffing firm. National firms also benefit from sheer inertia that permits them to retain customers despite less-than-optimal performance and service. Of course, larger firms also have had the advantage of more and larger VOP programs in place that made changing suppliers even more difficult for customers. Size matters.

However, there is an exception. When local firms aspire to growth by becoming regional or national and develop uniform standards, they may lose their local edge and start losing some of that business to local competitors. Talented individual recruiters insightful enough to identify a profitable service niche and astute enough not to incur excessive overhead in offices or staff have done very well filling gaps left by larger, traditional, standardized staffing firms.

How do firms grow geographically? It's all about the branches. It's also all about supply and demand. Staffing firms can build new branches around a great employee or manager or around an expanding customer. Staffing firms grow by opening branches and replicating their unique processes, software systems, and quality control methods in those new cities. It takes as few as two experienced people to open a new branch: a salesperson and an operations/service person.

The smartest regional companies that are expanding nationally tend to expand where they already have customers. When a customer expands, its staffing firms can expand with it. The customer's staffing assignments in a new city form a base of business from which to grow. When a staffing firm gets an assignment with a customer that has facilities in regions not yet served by the staffing firm, the firm can prospect strategically for new assignments in those regions. This is a demand side growth driver.

A supply side growth driver happens when a staffing firm finds ways to scaffold the establishment of new offices. One approach to scaffolding relies on a great employee who has a personal reason to move to another city. When a great salesperson or manager has personal reasons to want to move to another city or region, the staffing firm can build a new office around that person.

Another approach to scaffolding takes advantage of the staffing firm's ability to sell larger contracts than it can fulfill on its own and then to build alliances to fulfill them. Staffing firms sometimes conceal from the customer the fact that they cannot fill a large order. Staffing firms need to develop a network of trust with other suppliers. They may meet local suppliers at national staffing industry meetings. They may also turn to larger staffing firms to fill the orders; but this is less safe because those competitors could do it all and steal the business from them.

The key is to have met local suppliers in remote markets via national or international conferences or to join networks whose exclusive purpose is to assist collaboration among independent staffing agencies. Such networks help local staffing firms act like regional or national firms. Most such collaborations have not been particularly effective in serving true national business. The problem is that each individual company is incentivized to take as much from such a network as it can and rely on the other companies to invest in the network's infrastructure.

As discussed in chapter 2, personal relationships play a large role in both the supply and demand scenarios. Great staffing firms build great relationships and exploit them.

Why local firms become regional or national

Local firms find it tempting to become regional and regional firms find it tempting to go national. That's because they know size matters, because regional or national contracts represent more business, and because local service providers can't service those contracts as well as regional or national firms do.

Local service providers are perfectly capable of establishing networks or alliances to service regional or national business. However, the sense of purpose is diluted somewhat if the local company does not service the customer across its entire reach. In the alliance arrangement, the burden of failure for the suppliers is distributed and diffuse. This is in marked contrast to the national firms, where corporate officers can hold a branch manager accountable.

Similarly, when a local firm is asked to service national business that it did not originally sell, its motivation is usually less and its prioritization lower. The local firm is less likely to assign its best workers to someone else's customers even though it is being compensated for the service. As an added disincentive, the national customer is probably paying a lower bill rate for its workers than local customers are.

To counter this, a primary staffing supplier can apply incentives or penalties to ensure compliance by other suppliers. No company likes to lose business, even if the customer isn't its own or as profitable as its core business.

However, regional and national firms usually can do better because they can use their chain of command to keep branches aligned with the firm's regional or national priorities. That is why most regional and national contracts go to regional or national staffing firms.

How they expand

The first step that a local firm can take to become a regional supplier is looking at the existing customer base to determine whether they have needs elsewhere in the country. The other is the classic VOP model — to establish VOP programs locally for national customers and expand them once the relationship has proven itself. Local firms responding to distant RFPs have rarely been successful. As always, it's all about the relationship.

Most local firms expand by opening new branches before they find a customer in the new location. Most of these new branches struggle for their existence. It is much safer to open new branches after landing a regional or national contract that must be serviced from those locations. This base of business provides a viable foundation for the branch to grow.

Frequently, when a strong sales or service representative was leaving the company to go to a different city, usually due to a lifestyle change or trailing a spouse, Jay used it as an opportunity to open a remote office where that individual was going and made her/him the branch manager. This person knew the system, could be trusted, and shared the common values of the staffing firm. It's a much less risky procedure than flying in to a new market and hiring new people after random interviews. Not only did this prevent a good employee from going to a competitor, it also opened a new market.

An additional strategy that has been used by certain entrepreneurial firms is to establish a "business development relationship" with non-competitive staffing firms located in cities in which they desire to have a presence. In such a relationship, the firms share business with varying arrangements and splits. They get the advantage of "local coverage" in targeted parts of the country.

The downside to expansion

Theoretically, a national staffing supplier is a nationwide group of branch offices that are equally adept at servicing local and national business. But in reality, there are often differences in the servicing requirements, and perhaps more importantly, in the priorities assigned to local as opposed to national business. While a national staffing supplier is capable of providing excellent service to local customers, it likely will give the best service to its largest national customers.

It is tempting to declare that to succeed, each branch of a national staffing firm need only treat a national customer as if it were a local customer at that branch location — tempting but simplistic. It usually does not work that way. Companies in any industry tend to take care of their largest customers first. Even though national customers may be able to bargain for lower prices, their business may represent a lot more overall profit to the staffing firm than a smaller, local customer.

For national staffing suppliers, that might show up as a supervisor sending the better worker to a national customer. Or a national customer may have a sudden large-volume need that temporarily overwhelms the office. During that rush, that local office might not have the time to provide the appropriate level of service to a local customer.

Of course, a large local customer may also get the best treatment from a national staffing firm simply because it represents a lot of bread and butter to the firm.

How national firms can go international or global

National firms going international is a much greater stretch than regional firms going national. Despite the obstacles, many national firms have elected to do so or have felt compelled to do so by their largest customers. Today, there are surprisingly few large national customers that do not also have international operations. As such, it is increasingly awkward for a national firm to tell large international or global customers that it can fulfill only their national, not their international needs. Most international companies through their purchasing operations are more inclined to solicit a single global staffing supplier for ease of administration, preferential treatment, and best rates.

The path of least resistance for national suppliers to go international has been through their largest customers. Because staffing suppliers in general are doing an increasing percentage of their overall business with their largest customers (as might be anticipated from the classic 80/20 rule), it is tempting to follow the demand track throughout the world. Existing customers in mutually beneficial relationships with staffing suppliers are more likely to "take a chance" with these favored suppliers globally, even in countries where the supplier does not have a base.

Unfortunately, the move from national to international is a qualitative, as well as quantitative leap for all staffing suppliers. Because of extraordinary differences in labor laws and culture, staffing firms need to customize their operations in virtually every country. As such, separate, international divisions are required with expertise in each country's government regulations, taxation policy, employment law, and human resource management practices. This is not an insignificant investment for national staffing firms initiating international operations.

This is true even when the customer has a global operation. We make a distinction between international and global. An international operation may simply involve independent divisions in different countries. In a global operation, the customer has cross-national teams or divisions that operate as a single unit across countries. The global customer would prefer that the staffing firm's operations be seamless across international boundaries. But local politics, economics, and customs make that challenging.

International operations can be buffeted by powerful political winds. Soon after the turn of the century, the wars in Afghanistan and Iraq resulted in a huge opportunity for international staffing firms to pay workers well to work in the war zone. When security became an issue, riots erupted in the workers' home country — right outside the offices of a well-respected staffing firm. Some countries that bring in temporary workers keep them for such a long time that their children raise citizenship issues. In some cases, this results in painful political battles and stateless children who are not citizens of either their parents' land of origin or the country in which they were born.

International and global firms usually face internal politics, as well. Even when American executives in companies with a base in the United States think that they are bending over backward to accommodate the needs of managers and workers in other countries, managers from the other countries often feel like second-class citizens. This is likely to be true of international and global companies with a base in any location. People who work at the company's center of gravity simply have more pull. On the other hand, the high cost of initiating and maintaining international operations sometimes results in a diversion of resources and profits from home-base operations.

Whether a staffing firm is considering going from local to regional, regional to national, or national to international, the advantages of growth are compelling. With each leap in size, however, the firm loses certain competitive advantages at the local level and faces a new set of challenges. Staffing firms that manage those challenges well enough succeed handsomely.

The Challenges of Multiple Brands

Many large firms have developed multiple service lines. Some firms, such as Robert Half, have succeeded in developing a consistent layer of branding across multiple service lines. However, firms that branch out into service lines that differ significantly must develop different brands for each service line or each kind of service line. High-volume firms have been successful with adding a specialty brand. However, most specialists have found offering a high-volume brand less successful. There is an art to positioning and juggling multiple brands within a company. These challenges result in market gaps between large firms' brands that small firms can exploit to create profitable niche markets.

How can high-volume firms add a specialty brand? This takes place typically in response to specific requests by a customer, often one that has a VOP in place. The VOP supplier can choose to use backup specialty suppliers or to use this opportunity to grow their own specialty niche. In this situation, experienced staffing consultants can be especially effective. Sometimes, a high volume firm adds a specialty brand by acquiring a smaller niche operator as a way to gain the expertise necessary to be effective.

The most competitive firms segment internal operations. For both credibility reasons (i.e., branding) and for operational reasons, it is best not to use the same people to work on both high-volume and specialty engagements. In a VOP, the same person might oversee both high-volume and specialty workers but one group would recruit and evaluate the specialty workers and another group would recruit and evaluate the high-volume workers. We say more about segmenting marketing and operations in the next section on maintaining multiple brands.

It's less often that a specialist successfully adds a high-volume brand. Specialists invest a lot in grooming a high-value image. Adding a high-volume brand is usually inconsistent with this image. While a few specialist firms have built high-volume operations, they did so with a powerful market segmentation strategy that kept their specialty brand intact.

Maintaining multiple brands

When staffing firms add service lines that require different ways of operating and require employees with different skill sets, they find themselves juggling multiple brands both inside the organization and in the minds of customers.

Many general office service staffing firms have elected to expand into specialty services by naively creating a "separate division" named after that specialty service. Thus, a staffing firm creates an accounting division, a medical services division, a technical services division, etc. This rarely works. The marketplace is more skeptical and does not accept transformations that appear to be in name only.

The staffing firms that have been most successful in extending their service lines recognize this reality. They have created truly distinct divisions with different locations, staff, management, and marketing campaigns. Having a different location enables a new division to develop a different culture and expertise unique to that service line. The match between the marketing message and the internal distinctions allows the new division to develop the appropriate image in customers' minds.

Not having a different location creates the impression that a general staffing firm is "stretching" to incorporate areas of expertise that it has not truly mastered. Customers quickly see through an accounting desk, a medical and health services desk, a technical services desk, etc. It is not that the individuals who run these desks are unskilled (although they may be), but rather that it creates a difficult image to overcome in the minds of customers of a specialty staffing organization with no more depth than a single desk — or even a roomful of desks.

In fairness, it should be noted that on the executive search and full-time placement side of the business, such specialty desks are an acceptable practice. This is because a single, very capable individual can run the desk essentially without support and thus, unlike the traditional, temporary staffing side of the business, does not have to rely on an operational and service support that is generic to all staffing efforts.

Naming a specialty division of a generic staffing firm also creates confusion in the minds of customers, a definite no-no in marketing. The customers need to separate the specialty service from the perceived mediocrity of its generic roots. This is the same challenge that Toyota faced when it started its Lexus division. The public initially questioned spending extra money for a car that everyone understood was an upgraded Toyota Cressida. Eventually, however, the buying public became comfortable spending a lot more for a "Lexus," *not* a "Toyota Lexus."

Branding Works Differently in Executive Search

In executive search, the recruiter himself or herself can embody a brand. Customers pay a large premium to find a needle in a haystack — maybe an executive who speaks English, Hebrew and Hindi, has excellent skills at managing American, Israeli, and Indian workers, and has experience in high-end graphic design. The pool of potential candidates may be small and they may all be happy and successful at their current jobs and in no mood for a change. One or two recruiters can work at finding the few candidates who could be persuaded to take a look at the opportunity and help choreograph the dance in which customer and candidates get to know each other.

On the candidate side, the recruiter helps build interest as the candidate gets to know their potential hiring managers and colleagues. On the customer side, the recruiter helps the customer learn as much as they can — perhaps more than they would have noticed during interviews. In both cases, emotions can fog candidates' and customers' judgment — "Why didn't they call? They're not really interested, are they?" — and cause perfectly good matches to fall apart. Excellent recruiters can step in to untie the knots of misunderstandings and massage the negotiation process.

While specialty contingent staffing firms can learn from skilled executive recruiters, they are unlikely to be able to implement the intensive and expensive processes that work well when the stakes and the fee are so high. In contingent staffing, brands are embodied in divisions or whole organizations rather than in individual recruiters.

It may be easier to go in the other direction: A firm with a reputation for high quality can extend that reputation to new service lines. The danger here is the potential for diluting a good name. Robert Half is a good example of a very competitive and highly regarded specialized staffing firm that was originally positioned exclusively in the accounting and financial services segment of the market but successfully transformed itself into a more full-service office-staffing supplier. What is particularly impressive is that it exploited its fine reputation in a difficult service line to attract customers to its new line extensions — *without* undermining its core business position in accounting and financial services.

Effective training, recruitment, selection and reorientation of its employees — as well as clever market segmentation were all keys to its transformation and expansion. While Robert Half extended its classy image, it did what Toyota did in their marketing. It gave new names to its new divisions and kept them separate in the public mind. For instance, a simple Internet search for Robert Half in 2006 produced only Robert Half Finance & Accounting.

Exploiting Competitive Advantages

A large firm may find it too costly to service all of its accounts and meet its profit margin goals. Large firms usually have the advantage of being able to service most of a large customer's needs, while a smaller firm cannot. The large firm can be internally honest about the true costs associated with each account and use opportunistic strategies to embed itself in large customers that are profitable.

The firm can enmesh its proprietary systems with the client's, refuse to support other suppliers, and expand its service offerings so it can cover *all* of a client's staffing needs. Such a leader might even suggest to sales staff that they should not go after accounts where the firm doesn't enjoy a competitive advantage. Instead, they can focus sales efforts on a targeted segment of the market and increase the percentage of closes in that target market. After the engagement is finalized, the firm can assign specific people to retain the business and make the new client a "customer for life."

Small firms, on the other hand, can exploit a market niche into which they have special insight. Talented individual recruiters who went off on their own and who were insightful enough to identify a profitable service niche and astute enough not to incur excessive overhead, either in their offices or with their staffs, did very well during the last decade. There is probably a lesson here for all staffing firms. First-mover advantage wins a niche, so long as the supplier is not too far ahead of the curve. Trying to supply something before the demand is really there is a setup for failure. With the mass retirement of the baby boom generation, a vast number of niches are emerging.

Often, changing technology creates niches that a nimble firm can exploit. For instance, when many companies start implementing a new software package that requires special skills to configure or use, people with those skills become high in demand. When there are too few people to place, the search costs may be too high for this service line to be profitable, but as the number of available workers grows or if a staffing firm is able to situate itself so as to attract workers with these skills, this specialty service line can become very lucrative.

Another case of this comes when the supply source cuts off. For instance, the Navy has trained a steady stream of technicians and engineers in boiler technology. Upon leaving the service, these men and women found that they had the right skills to work in power plants that used similar technology. When the Navy began switching to something different, power plant managers worried about the future supply of trained labor. Such a looming shortage provides an opportunity for a staffing firm with a solution.

The importance of focus

Imaginative leaders may notice many potential competitive advantages and envision how to exploit them. While going after several at once may seem enticing, the best companies know where to focus. Even those companies that have managed to branch out into many areas successfully have often taken time to do so or have developed flexible internal cultures that few can match.

In chapter 1, we discussed the five success factors for effective organizational change. Implementing each exacts a cost. For instance, leaders who excel in describing their new vision may have to work hard to build internal political support for the vision or find themselves tugging hard to motivate people to want to change at all. Once those are in place, management structures must created and set in motion to execute the change program. Competitive firms know where their strengths are and spend the time and effort to invest in building the other foundations for successful change. They don't try to implement more changes at one time than their internal processes and culture can handle.

Whether a staffing firm aims to shift from local to regional operations, to open a new division to take advantage of a change in the market, or to exploit some other competitive advantage, it must consider the internal capabilities required to go after this new opportunity and conduct a realistic self-assessment of its readiness to deploy such capabilities. Only then can it turn great ideas into successful outcomes.

Chapter Five

EXPLOITING TECHNOLOGY

Computers and software have dramatically altered the staffing landscape. They have provided staffing firms with a global reach not possible a few decades ago. They have given rise to new services that would have made for good science fiction in the early days of the staffing industry.

The acceptance of software has similarly changed dramatically over time. And as younger generations — raised on ubiquitous cell phones and online social networks — flood the workplace, the role of technology will change. This will bring a new set of challenges.

Once, even the idea of office automation was dreaded. Jonathan recalls his experience with early office automation using IBM PCs when they were new and — depending on your perspective — exciting or frightening. The software developer was building office automation software from scratch, relying on users to inform him about their business processes and the ways in which automation could improve productivity. Back then, even experienced computer users often found it difficult to describe their processes and reporting needs clearly. And most of the users had no idea how computers could help them. Many clients believed that standardizing their processes sounded like something that would tie their hands. Some who were new to computing even worried that the computers might blow up (literally), because that is what they had seen in movies. Many worried — more legitimately — that their jobs would go away if they participated in office automation. You can imagine the emotional tone of meetings with managers whose operations were about to be automated!

Today, computer users have a lot of experience, but they still want flexibility in their business processes and in software that supports them. Developers often find themselves trying to offer a large number of options to users. Options are attractive when customization is easy, but even then, staffing firms must have enough in-house expertise to configure all of those options.

We have found that users' experience of software differs dramatically based on their level of computer knowledge. Because user-friendliness is in the eye of the beholder, what we say in this chapter will match only some users' experience. As an example, we know some people whose knowledge about a particularly well-known software package differs so much that one calls it user-friendly while the other imagines that the software development team must have spent most of its time finding insidious ways to annoy its users.

People often approach technology as a set of features they need. That causes them to lose sight of two things: how well the technology supports the company and unintended consequences from this technology. Highly competitive staffing firms select technology strategically and examine the risk of unintended consequences before making their selections. In other words, they select outcomes, not features. They select for desired outcomes and they mitigate the adverse consequences.

Technology develops over time, making old processes work faster and new services possible that we could only dream of years ago. Staffing firms face a myriad of technological choices that develop and proliferate over time. Which technology is most effective for a specific firm differs depending on a variety of factors, including the relationships between staffing firms and their backup suppliers and between staffing firms and their customers, the volume of a service line, and labor market balance.

Consider three ways in which technology can be used to support staffing firms: as a support to strategy — including providing services to customers and contingent workers, as a means to boost efficiency of existing processes, and for customers to keep control over staffing suppliers and costs. Technology allows fewer people to accomplish more in less time and allows access to information that enables better management of staffing processes.

Vendor management systems (VMSs) at first enabled staffing firms to streamline project management with backup suppliers. Later, customers began to use it to substitute for vendor-on-premises (VOP) programs.

In high-volume service lines, technology such as candidate matching software and Web-based testing automates a complex process so that it can be done repeatedly without adding much extra cost.

In low-volume service lines, technology is more costly and less efficient unless the base cost can be absorbed by a staffing firm's existing high-volume operations.

In this chapter, we do not address specific software packages because they are always changing. Instead, we address some underlying principles that can provide some direction for dealing with a wide variety of software packages over time. We also expect that Web 2.0 innovations and mobile wireless platforms will change the equation even further. Both technological innovations involve a radical change in culture as much as they involve software development. So, as a new generation of virtually adept workers and managers tied to global communities rises in the workforce, we expect that new relationships between people, work and technology will alter the staffing industry dramatically.

Technology's Promises and Unintended Consequences

Here is what technology can do for you: It can boost the efficiency and transparency of your existing systems. You can use it to wow your customers. It can even become the basis for entirely new and exciting (and risky) business models. But ill-conceived or poorly implemented technology can drag a company down. We discuss both the promises of technology and the risks, and offer suggestions for mitigating those risks.

Promises promises

Purveyors of technology make many promises for what their hardware and software can do for staffing firms. Some require little change in current operations, while others involve remaking the business. The promises fall into a few categories:

- increased efficiency and lower cost,
- improvements in service delivery,
- new types of service delivery that provide a clear competitive advantage, and
- enhanced decision-making by employees.

Increasing efficiency

Efficiency-boosting software that is prevalent in the staffing industry includes sourcing and candidate matching programs as well as programs that integrate with heavily used front- and back-office software. These include email, word processing, scheduling and timecard, payroll, and ERP software. In addition, most competitive firms use software to assess contingent workers' skills and to track and document their performance. Some may also use programs to track staffing firm employee performance.

Local firms planning to go regional or national require scalable systems. At the extreme, some cheap candidate-matching software late in the 20th century was able to search for skills, but not for both skills and locale. The ability to work over the Web also has made software more scalable.

In high-volume service lines, technology such as candidate-matching software and Web-based testing automates a complex process so that it can be done repeatedly without adding much extra cost. In low-volume service lines, technology is more costly and less efficient unless the base cost can be absorbed by a staffing firm's existing high-volume operations. In firms that specialize in low-volume lines, the benefits of technology come from the way software can find a needle in a haystack more than from its efficiencies.

Providing services through technology

As discussed in previous chapters, staffing firms can use software to provide job skills testing and training for contingent workers, career coaching, and support for contingent workers' job searches.

Competitive staffing firms provide a whole gamut of online and computer-based training, especially in office support and clerical areas. This includes training in how to use standard office software packages, customer service skills, and orientation to a wide variety of organizations and functions. Sometimes, staffing firms purchase the training programs directly and offer them online. At other times, they subscribe to online training services that provide a huge range of training titles online.

For career coaching, some software packages provide self-assessments to help contingent workers increase their sense of career direction and expand their horizons with additional options.

Staffing firms increasingly provide user-friendly sites for contingent workers to conduct searches for assignments that fit them. This is both a service to contingent workers and an efficiency measure for the staffing firm because it empowers contingent workers to conduct searches for whatever positions appeal to them. And it makes staffing representatives' work that much easier.

Exploiting technology to wow the customer

Firms that invest in technology that makes useful information available to their customers can get an edge over their competitors. Consider the "Wow!" factor.

Customers are demanding rapid ability to generate customized status, usage and cost reports. Such reports enable them to better manage their HR budgets and staff. For instance, they can see the range of rates being paid to various vendors for similar positions across the company and either standardize those rates or give managers flexibility to raise rates for highly specialized contingent staff. Historically, these reports were very labor intensive for the staffing supplier. Sophisticated suppliers today are able to generate a wide range of permutations and combinations of reporting options in most configurations that customers might require with little or no additional programming.

Software that provides customers with a true paperless system is also welcome. Cutting paperwork can unburden HR and purchasing staff tremendously and allow them to focus on more strategic issues.

Making HR and purchasing people look good in front of senior management helps keep customers. Great software gives them information that they can put into flashy presentations, that they can use to instantly answer probing questions about "How many?", "How much?", and "By when?" HR has not historically been good at providing financial analysis without support from the accounting department or others with access to good information. A strong VMS package can make them much more self-sufficient and responsive.

Staffing firms themselves can use similar tactics in sales presentations to customers, showing customers information about themselves that even they didn't know.

Driving decision-making downward

Driving decision-making to employees within the staffing firm can increase efficiency and customer service. In order for employees to make decisions that used to be the purview of management, they need access to information and training on how to gather and analyze that information and use it to make decisions.

This is more challenging than simply providing employees with software or using software to wow a customer. Most top managers complain that their frontline managers and employees lack adequate problem-identification and problem-solving skills. Top managers are usually knowledgeable enough to look at information about a situation and quickly see what kinds of problems might be inherent in that situation. They do not understand that employees given the same information usually do not recognize the same patterns in that information.

Ongoing training and mentoring are needed to help employees develop proficiency in recognizing patterns and problems and begin the problem-solving process. Staffing firms that excel in preparing employees to utilize information and make quick, effective decisions can be much more nimble than staffing firms that cannot do so. The top-heavy firms require a lot more time for information to be aggregated from frontline employees and databases, for top managers to meet and make decisions, and then for the managers to communicate those decisions and delegate action back to the employees.

Driving decision-making to contingent workers can be a strategic move to make the firm more attractive as well as more efficient. Technology can enable contingent workers to self-select assignments more quickly and possibly with more accurate matching. This gives contingent workers a sense of greater empowerment and commitment to the staffing firm because the firm helps them to control their own destinies. With quicker and more accurate matching, customers and contingent workers experience more successful outcomes. And with high enough volume, the cost of technology implementation is offset by reductions in matching costs.

How far can staffing firms go with technology? They can go all the way — so that technological innovations become the core of their strategy.

Technology-driven business models

Technology has enabled some exciting business models to be attempted that weren't possible in the years before the Internet caught on. While some of these models may have failed in the past, that failure should not stop new people from trying them again with some modifications or new approaches. That is because these innovative business models promise to revolutionize the relationships between staffing companies and their customers, backup suppliers, and employees. We describe three models: virtual sourcing — which is the least risky and easiest to try — virtual matchmaking, and virtual *everything*.

Virtual sourcing. Social networking sites, blogs and other recent business tools being dubbed Web 2.0 have been changing the experience of life for tens of millions of people worldwide. Virtual communities have been formed where people can get to know each other based on common interests and expertise rather than geography. A tech employer in Palo Alto, Calif., might meet a programmer from Bucharest, Romania, and chat for weeks as part of a social/technological group and discover some common interests. A few months later, the employer needs someone with the programmer's skills and hires that person to move across oceans and continents.

More recently, Web-based portals are emerging. Staffing companies can set up their own virtual offices or career fairs, and interview candidates via such a Web portal.

Enterprising staffing firms are using similar methods for virtual sourcing. The most competitive staffing firms have good intelligence on what skills are about to be in high demand and low supply. They send savvy staff onto blogs and chat rooms to communicate with people whose skills are soon to be a match for the labor market. After getting to know them and evaluating their skill sets and interpersonal proficiency, they can reel them in for hard-to-fill positions.

A Web 2.0-savvy staffing firm can develop quite a reputation worldwide within an online community of professionals who work in a particular service line — preferably a reputation for being effective at placing people with particular skill sets. This would help that firm to corner a niche in the labor market in ways that geographically-challenged staffing companies can only dream of.

That should be a warning to currently competitive staffing firms whose service lines are about to be disrupted by virtually savvy players anywhere on the planet.

Virtual matchmaking. Jay worked as the VP of marketing for a well-funded dot-com startup whose business model was to match staffing firms that had job orders they could not fill with staffing firms that had candidates they could not place. This highly-automated, Web-based system worked fabulously. However, like many dot-com startups, the firm burned through a lot of cash.

The business was based on a "co-opetition" model whereby competitors would collaborate to close deals that they could not close on their own. Many firms shied away from this due to mutual distrust and being technology-averse. They feared sharing information lest it give away some of their perceived competitive advantage. And the Internet was still too new for this business model to capture their imaginations. For this business model to succeed, we would have needed to gather a critical mass of both job orders and candidates — a mass large enough to create a profitable volume of matches.

We were ahead of the curve. And this business model can be tried again when a larger number of staffing firms are tech-savvy and more comfortable with co-opetition.

Virtual everything. Jay also worked as the COO of a virtual staffing company that aimed to recruit anyone in office support positions who could work virtually for our customers. The sourcing, testing, training and the work itself were to be done over the Internet using proprietary software. Confidentiality was highly guarded. Intellectual property was protected by having all work done on a secure server whereby content could not be downloaded, even by the person working on the document. The client company's identity was typically hidden from the contingent worker. Tasks were broken up among multiple contingent workers to further aid in security and speed of processing.

The only thing that got in our way was the dot-com crash. After the economic recovery in the early years of the new century, this kind of work has become commonplace in outsourcing, but not yet in the staffing industry. By the time you read this book, someone may have succeeded using this business model. Otherwise, our entrepreneurial readers are encouraged to go after this opportunity.

Unintended consequences

Thankfully, most technology implementations don't involve risking the entire firm. But technology's unintended consequences can range from little annoyances to significant harm to the bottom line. A range of adverse consequences associated with technology implementation represent potential threats to the health of the firm. Staffing companies must balance desired outcomes with unintended consequences, such as unexpectedly high training costs, software instability, and competitive advantages blunted due to natural organizational resistance to change.

Software development and implementation involve a series of tradeoffs. Each balances desired outcomes with unintended consequences. Staffing firms that use technology wisely manage these tradeoffs well.

Many managers budget for software purchases without adequately budgeting for training. The learning curve makes new software expensive to implement. The price of hardware and software is small compared to the expense of training and dislocation that happens when jobs must be redesigned to fit the software. When users complain that software is not user-friendly, it may be a sign that they lack the needed training. Their complaints may be a result of a steep learning curve or simply not having budgeted enough for training.

Innovative firms sometimes develop new processes that are not supported by existing software. Software developers can't develop features to fit each firm's specific processes, so staffing firms face a choice: invest in customizing software, develop workarounds that enable them to continue working with software that doesn't truly match their processes, or standardize their processes.

Two areas in which this can be an issue are report generation and integration with back-office software. In reporting, the problem is that standardized reports produced by staffing software may not match a particular staffing firm's unique processes. These issues arise with many kinds of software, not just those related to staffing. They occur most often with firms that have their own special way of doing things.

Larger firms can afford to have reports customized to meet their needs. Small firms may find themselves choosing between standardizing their processes to fit the software and creating workarounds.

Software developers that try to meet the needs of all the varied processes used by different staffing firms may find themselves producing software bloat. That is where developers keep adding more features until users have to navigate through too many menus to find the functions they use most often. Staffing firms that select software based mostly on features also drive software bloat.

Progressive staffing firms might find it exciting to be on the leading edge, but software instability can make being on the "bleeding edge" of technology quite painful. Repeated software crashes frustrate workers. Software crashes that lose data make them go through the roof. Poorly tested and debugged new features can crash the software. Software developers sometimes put out such software because they added or modified so many features that they ran out of time and felt pressure to bring it to market ahead of competitors' software upgrades or customers' expectations.

On the other end of the spectrum, some software developers focus so much on software stability that they take years to make the leap to new platforms. For instance, some software didn't make the shift from DOS to Windows or to the Web for more than a decade after their competitors took the leap. Some résumé software could not read HTML résumés years after everyone started using Web-based job posting systems. Staff had to retype those résumés or put them through special programs that turned HTML résumés into text-only documents.

There are more change management hazards besides steep learning curves and aligning software features with business operations. Any time a company changes its processes, workers go through the challenge of changing habits and reacting emotionally to the loss of comfort with the way things worked. In chapter 1, we talked about the importance of communicating the rationale for decisions when they are important, unexpected, or negative; we also reviewed the success factors for change that leaders must make sure are in place. Not ensuring the presence of those success factors is a recipe for resistance. People resist change unless they are motivated and have the needed support systems.

IT departments usually budget well for software implementation and some even budget well for training. But few also budget enough for the change management work. And top managers often don't realize how much they need to communicate to the organization when changing processes or technology or how much effort they need to put into the five success factors for change discussed in chapter 1, Leading People. One story is told about a well-respected technology company that put computers into hospitals to track all data critical to the business enterprise. Top management at the client had not involved the nurses during the planning stage and had not discovered that there was no room at many nurses' workstations for computers. Without the up-front dialogue, the system design was flawed. When word got out that computers were being implemented, nurses refused to use them. Millions of dollars were spent for a system that went dark.

A more subtle, unintended consequence occurs when too many companies in an industry implement a system successfully. For instance, recruiters' success with online social media may result in a flood of job postings that overwhelm online discussion groups. This can lead to frustration among group members who want to focus on discussion of substantive issues. The risk is that people may stop using those discussion groups or spend much less time on the whole social network.

Technology holds out so many promises, but also delivers so many challenges that some companies rack up unexpectedly large costs and don't realize half the potential benefits. Technology implementations can also hinder — or help — relationships with backup suppliers and customers. We consider the promises and unintended consequences of those in the next section.

Relationships Should Influence Technology Choices

Technology can help staffing firms provide services more efficiently to their customers. At the same time, it also affects the power balance relationships between staffing firms and customers. Just as vendor-on-premises (VOP) programs help link a staffing firm into a customer's system, staffing firms can use technology to tighten their hold on customers. Large customers often use technology — VMS systems — to increase their power and gain control over their staffing vendors.

Similarly, technology affects VOP staffing firm's relationships with backup suppliers. Tuning the technology to put backup suppliers at a disadvantage can have consequences on the suppliers' willingness to work with the VOP staffing firm. That, in turn, can have an adverse impact on the relationship with the customer.

Staffing firms should choose how to exploit technology with the health of those critical relationships in mind.

Customers are being pitched both by staffing suppliers — typically VOP operators — and by VMS providers to install VMSs. VOP operators usually want customers to accept their proprietary VMS software and usually provide it at no cost to their VOP customers. VMS providers charge customers to install and manage software that they claim will save customers a lot of money, make relationships with multiple staffing vendors more transparent and easier to manage, and reduce the cost of recruiting contingent workers. In theory, all of these benefits should accrue to both kinds of VMSs, those provided by staffing suppliers and those provided by VMS vendors directly to customers.

On being neutral

VMS software provided by VMS development companies is by definition vendor neutral. However, VMS software provided by VOP staffing suppliers may not be.

Should VMS software provided by VOP staffing suppliers be vendor-neutral? There are two perspectives on this: Yes and No.

Suppliers that say no typically do so in order to maximize their short-term gain. They may not recognize it as short-term, but in our next section, we describe the dynamics that make it short-term. If disclosed, there is not an ethical issue, here, but rather a business decision.

Suppliers are likely to gain a disproportionate share of the contingent workforce budget by building in a preferential advantage, typically with respect to when they receive the order. Non-neutrality means that all secondary suppliers will be considered only after the VOP program finds itself unable to fill an order in a reasonable period of time. That is a possible arrangement, and there's nothing improper about it — as long as it is disclosed to all backup suppliers as well as to the customer. Full disclosure to everyone is essential if the supplier is to keep everyone's trust.

Even in this case, it is beneficial for the VOP provider to treat all backup suppliers in a neutral manner, i.e., informing them all at the same time and with the same high-quality information.

Why neutrality matters

It's a matter of trust. VOP staffing suppliers often claim that their vendor management software is "vendor neutral" — that all backup staffing suppliers have the same opportunity to fill the customer's assignment orders. Should staffing firms running VOP programs make such claims? Will customers believe them?

Full disclosure and trust make a difference for backup suppliers, customers, and the staffing firm that runs the VOP program.

Why would backup suppliers agree to anything less than complete vendor neutrality? Typically, because they want the business. And as staffing companies themselves, they will understand that the VOP supplier incurs all the administrative costs. But that doesn't mean they will accept being put at a disadvantage to their direct competitors.

Why would customers care about this issue? Because savvy customers know that the quality of contingent workers provided by secondary suppliers is often a function of the priority they ascribe to a particular customer. That priority is likely to depend on backup suppliers' perception of the fairness of treatment that they receive from the primary vendor and their opportunity to compete for business.

Why should primary suppliers be so concerned about how much backup suppliers trust them? The reality is that no primary supplier, on premises or not, can fill all the staffing needs of a customer, especially a large one, all of the time. Thus it is essential that the primary supplier establish a network to round out the supply of candidates. This is easier said than done; it requires finesse and diplomacy to get it to work smoothly in a way that is seamless to all staffing users, whoever is coordinating it.

The psychology behind trust

As discussed in chapter 4, VOP providers rely on backup suppliers to make the customer happy. The trick is to motivate all backup suppliers not only to send properly qualified workers as needed and with minimal lead times, but also to get them to send their better workers. Here again, the key issue is trust.

The primary supplier has to trust that the backup suppliers will perform for it but not try to steal the customer. The backup suppliers have to trust that the primary supplier will allow them to fill a reasonable amount of profitable orders and also not steal its contingent workers (also called temp-napping). Only that will motivate them to remain a supplier of someone else's customer.

It is possible for a VOP operator to provide a technology platform and a set of business processes that are vendor-neutral, but it has little incentive to do so. Typically, proprietary software used by a VOP will come with some advantage built in for it.

The advantage may be in the form of lead time before the order goes to backup suppliers, or of selective distribution, which leaks the order to favored backup suppliers so they can have a qualified candidate ready to present as soon as the order is officially placed. Again, there is nothing inherently wrong in allowing the VOP operator the advantage of filling the orders first, as long as all backup suppliers and the customer know this will happen.

The bottom line

The bottom line is that staffing firms can sell customers on VOP programs backed by relatively neutral and transparent rules of engagement by pointing out their superior expertise in contingent workforce staffing and showing that they will follow those rules. They can sell secondary suppliers on supporting the VOP with high quality contingent workers by giving each supplier equal opportunity to supply contingent workers when the primary supplier cannot do so in a short amount of time.

Shaping relationships with customers

Staffing customers purchase vendor management software from VMS providers or get it for free from staffing firms in VOP relationships. Wouldn't any customer gladly accept free vendor management software from its staffing supplier? Maybe not, if such a purportedly "free" gift comes with hidden costs and could incur future liabilities.

For instance, some free software comes with biases built in that favor the staffing firm that provided the software or that give the staffing supplier access to competitors' pricing information. Knowing this, some backup suppliers might refuse to participate when the customer needs them.

It is technically possible for a supplier to provide a platform and a set of business processes that are vendor-neutral, as discussed earlier.

More often, proprietary software provided by a staffing company will come with some favoritism or advantage for that specific supplier built in. The bias may be in the form of a specific amount of "lead time" before the order goes "wide" to other potential vendors, or selective distribution, or surreptitious "leakage" of the order to the supplying vendor's own branches or favored backup suppliers, with the result that they will have a qualified candidate ready to present as soon as the order is "officially" placed.

Resist temptation

What is the harm in the previous scenarios if orders are filled more rapidly? In addition to the possible ethical issues if the system's built-in bias isn't clearly understood by all involved, the lack of a level playing field serves to discourage the best staffing suppliers from working with the primary supplier. Inequitable practices, once discovered, turn off all but the most desperate and least qualified suppliers. Those are not the companies that anyone should rely on in a pinch.

Even so, it may be tempting for customers to take on such software — if it works well and is fully responsive to contingent staffing needs. But they won't want to be locked into using it forever, and they may not want it to be integrated inextricably with their order fulfillment processes. Unfortunately, some high-functioning systems are designed to do exactly that.

Customers may find it more tempting to accept free VMS software from a preferred supplier that has a good track record with that customer. Customers should be, but are often not, cautious about backup suppliers' *perceptions* about the fairness of the process. That is important because the ongoing performance effectiveness of the preferred supplier is always a function of the level of cooperation and trust that is developed with the back-up suppliers, which may be turned off by their perception of a biased VMS.

The good news is that there are things that your customers can do to protect themselves and still take advantage of "free" vendor management software. If you are a backup supplier to a customer that has taken these precautions, then you do not need to be as concerned.

First, customers can require their primary staffing supplier provide a truly vendor-neutral platform.

Second, customers can demand that the primary staffing supplier disclose what, if any, advantage it gains from providing free software, beyond good will. To do this, the customer should have received complete documentation and a flowchart of their order-filling process. Customers can negotiate with the primary staffing supplier to get assurances of backup suppliers' opportunity to bid in a way that protects the integrity of the process.

These items should be included in a detailed written agreement that describes the contractual terms and obligations of the parties associated with the use, installation and future removal of the vendor management software.

Why customers accept free VMS software

After allowing for the issues and cautions identified above, there may still be good reasons for a customer to accept free vendor management software.

First, it is free. By comparison, commercially available vendor management software can be costly and may entail perpetual license fees.

Second, it is staffing-customized. Much commercially available vendor management software is not specifically designed to work with staffing suppliers. It can be customized, but any user would prefer to have a staffing supplier do that at the staffing supplier's expense.

Third, it will be up to date. These systems are constantly being revised and updated. Why not have a staffing supplier do that for them as well?

Fourth, it has been tested. With software provided by staffing suppliers, testing is less likely to be an issue.

Fifth, it will usually be integrated by the staffing supplier into the customer's existing purchasing and accounting software. By doing so, suppliers can give themselves a retention advantage. Once their software systems become integrated into the client's software systems, the customer may find it difficult to shift suppliers.

Managers' relationships and decision quality

This demonstrates how software configurations can shape relationships between firms and their customers. Similarly, configurations for software packages used in-house also shape relationships, and the decision about which package to purchase and how to configure it should be made with a clear picture of the ideal relationships. What data get reported, how those reports look, and who receives the reports shapes the issues that staffing firm managers and employees focus on while determining how to do their work.

It's obvious that managers and employees who have access to key reports have more power than those who don't. Less obviously, certain decisions are easier to make when there is data to diagnose what is going on. A lack of data can lead to indecision or endless bickering among managers. Too much poorly organized data can lead to analysis paralysis. Even more insidious, one manager's opinion may be easier to support because reports show data that backs up his/her argument, but the data to back up the other side are simply not reported. Opportunistic and outspoken managers sometimes argue for reports to show their favorite data and exclude information that might not be in their favor.

Whether VMS software, financial packages, or recruiting software configuration is being discussed, executives should make sure that data-entry and reporting functions are configured to provide data on all critical decisions and in ways that support different opinions and better decisions rather than to tilt in favor of opportunistic managers' pet issues and opinions.

Summary

Technological innovations have created radical changes in the staffing industry and in the relationships between people and their work. Technology offers staffing firms some enticing advantages, but also comes with risks that some firms choose to ignore.

Highly competitive staffing firms typically select technologies based on cutting costs as well as strategic outcomes such as enhanced service delivery, efficiency, and management of backup suppliers, processes and costs. Technology can have other benefits such as improving staffing decision-making and giving rise to innovative business models that provide customers services that give the staffing firm a competitive edge.

On the other hand, staffing companies must balance these desirable outcomes with the adverse consequences of technology implementation, such as training costs and misalignments between software and strategy that can threaten the bottom line.

Vendor management software can support or hinder critical relationships by affecting the power balance between staffing suppliers and their customers. Transparency and neutrality are essential for helping to secure trust between customers and suppliers. Clearly stipulating the contractual terms for the use, installation, and removal of free VMS can reduce perceptions of a power imbalance and give staffing companies an advantage in terms of enhanced efficiency, cost, and strengthened customer-supplier relationships.

Similarly, any software that provides reports that managers need to make decisions can be tuned to help or hinder smooth relationships among managers and to make decisions easy or difficult to make. Technology and software configuration choices should be made with these considerations in mind.

Chapter Six

MITIGATING RISK

Risk management issues expanded and dominated profitability strategy agendas at most staffing firms in many states during the past decade. Our increasingly litigious business environment and higher jury awards in discrimination, harassment and retaliation lawsuits added urgency to risk management initiatives. The intricacies of co-employment liability exposure added complexity and ambiguity to these initiatives. And then there was a marked increase in litigation for negligent referencing, background checking, hiring, retention and supervision, to name just five.

Most staffing suppliers were hard-pressed to understand where their responsibility ended and their customers' due diligence and supervisory responsibility began. For example, whose responsibility was it when the vendor to a customer was accused of sexually harassing a contingent worker supplied by a staffing firm but supervised by the customer? Would the responsibility have shifted if the staffing firm had a VOP in place at the customer site, with an on-site manager provided by the staffing supplier? Not always easy questions to answer. Jay has often had the privilege of explaining these subtleties to a jury or opposing counsel.

As has often been the case, risk management proficiency was quickly turned into a competitive advantage by staffing firms that believed they had a positive story to share with their customers. In some arrangements, especially those characterized by a VOP, proactive staffing suppliers took some responsibility for the HR and risk management programs that transcended the workers whom they supplied to their customers.

These firms felt that they had effective programs in place to mitigate risk for their contingent workers that could easily be extended to their customers' direct employees as well. But not without incurring some additional potential liability exposure, in Jay's opinion. When asked, he always recommended against that practice. But sometimes the marketing utility took precedence.

In the last decade, there emerged a profitable niche in which specialized firms did more than merely offer risk management programs to their existing staffing customers. Taking advantage of the continuing national trend towards increased outsourcing of essential organizational functions, a number of firms moved into that space for the entire spectrum of HR functions, including of course, risk management. Judging by the earnings and stock appreciation of the public companies at least, these firms have done quite well. The niche and the need were real.

Highly competitive staffing firms manage the risks inherent in being one of two employers, never allowing critical responsibilities to fall through the cracks between vendor and customer. They look out for warning signs from customers and employees. That means welcoming messages that managers don't usually like to hear. They control the damage from low-performers within their firm. They monitor employee performance and reward the high-performers, not the low performers. They document low performance and terminate employees who consistently underperform.

They also avoid dysfunctional management practices and politics that all too many executives allow to flourish unchecked. And they work with customers to take advantage of opportunities to learn from contingent workers as they leave their last assignment. They use acceptable human resources practices and practice human resources risk management, but not so far as to become paralyzed by caution. They protect themselves from biased measurement systems, and use technical expertise from research in industrial-organizational psychology when rolling out employment tests, performance appraisals, and job interviews to predict and measure performance.

The Challenge of Co-employment

Contingent workers may be employed by a staffing firm, but they do their work under the supervision of a client company. According to our understanding of prevailing law, a client company cannot give contingent workers the same rewards and training that it gives to its employees or else the contingent workers' legal status as contingent could be challenged. This dual employment status creates some sticky legal issues and challenges in worker commitment:

Defining Co-employment

Legally referred to as a "joint employer" relationship, co-employment is often used to describe the relationship among two or more employers when each has specific actual or potential legal responsibilities to the same worker or group of workers, as determined by various employment agencies, including the EEOC.

We discuss three legal issues in later sections of this chapter:

1. How should a staffing firm handle legal violations that are the customer's creation, but could become the staffing firm's problem? For instance, equal employment opportunity and disability laws are the joint responsibility of both the staffing firm and the customer. Even if the customer commits an equal opportunity or disability violation, the staffing company needs to respond with the same speedy and thorough investigation that it would do if one of its own employees committed the violation.

2. Employees must be hired and terminated legally. If a customer asks a staffing firm to avoid hiring members of a protected class, such as women or minorities, the staffing firm is liable for discrimination if it follows through with the improper request.

3. Harassment should be prevented and *must* be responded to quickly and comprehensively. Reckless managers who harass their employees need to be quickly retrained or removed.

A customer's workers' compensation insurance usually does not cover contingent staff employed by a staffing firm. Staffing firms must make sure that they have adequate coverage for the contingent workers whom they dispatch to their customers.

How can customers keep contingent workers committed to their goals when the customer organization isn't paying them and cannot legally give them the same rewards and training as they give to employees? The best staffing firms develop consultative relationships with their customers to help customers surmount such motivational challenges. Often it entails a compromise between risk management and motivational objectives. At the very least, valid and reliable performance metrics must be in place and reviewed for all contingent workers.

Watch for early warning signs

Highly competitive staffing firms watch out for warning signs with customers and employees. Warning signs may come from customers themselves, such as when they voice complaints about expectations not met by the staffing firm, but they may come in the form of data, such as lower profit margins due to price wars or increasing attrition among employees due to poor management.

Staffing firms must make it easy for customers to discuss their perceptions of the staffing firm's work and for employees and contingent workers to voice their concerns. Staffing firm managers must also review quantitative and interview data that allow them to see trends that must be acted upon.

Heed warning signs from customers

Everyone knows that it costs much more to acquire a new customer than it costs to satisfy and retain a current customer. Many people believe that it costs 10 times more. The problem is that most staffing firms do not act on this sage advice even though they espouse it in training programs and at meetings. Staffing firms must listen well enough to customers to recognize when a customer feels that small problems are piling up without being solved. After enough of them accumulate, the customer will switch to another supplier.

One might imagine that customers switch due to a single, unfortunate incident, such as failing to supply critically needed contingent workers. However, such a failure need not result in the customer switching as long as the staffing firm notices early that this is happening and provides the customer with adequate notice that it cannot fill a key vacancy. Even when such a failure happens, a facile supplier may be able to own up to the problem, act quickly to correct it, and apologize, turning a negative into a positive. Customers differ dramatically in their willingness to forgive such lapses and to allow their suppliers to recover from their indiscretions.

More typically, a customer switches staffing firms because the staffing supplier takes the customer's business for granted and devotes its best efforts to acquiring new customers, not servicing it. Sometimes this neglect shows up as a perception of financial exploitation, such as when competitive industry prices continues to decline but the supplier holds steady or even begins to increase billing rates. At other times, a staffing firm's service deteriorates because it puts its best effort and best workers into newly acquired customers.

Motivation to change staffing suppliers sometimes comes from the outside, as well. Perhaps an aggressive backup supplier will approach the customer directly despite an agreement with the primary supplier not to do so. Usually, the backup supplier will make a case for eliminating middlemen and providing a slightly lower price. The ethics of this practice may be debated.

Alternatively, a staffing consultant or the customer's own purchasing department may conduct a review of staffing options and costs. While many in the staffing industry lament the increasing role that purchasing departments play in staffing supplier decisions, the reality is that they have become quite sophisticated in recent years and have the capacity to save customers considerable money when negotiating incremental staffing-related services. Astute staffing firms take the time to calculate what customers are likely to discover when they run a financial and strategic analysis of their contingent worker costs, quality, speed and service.

A harsh reality in some staffing relationships is that new business can be bought in a number of ways. Large staffing suppliers may determine that it is in their best interest to acquire certain large or particularly prestigious customers, despite their apparent ability to make money in those relationships. They presume that they will make up the apparent loss or small profit through leveraging the reputations of those large customers. Or, they may wish to take customers from competitors to show the value of their marketing schemes. The danger to staffing firms is that creating a price war can eliminate profitability. The danger to customers comes from the fact that paying low prices may put them low on the staffing firm's list of priorities.

Competitive staffing firms persuade customers that their billing rates are competitive given the value they provide; and when customers are approached by staffing firms with lower rates, highly competitive staffing firms persuade them that switching results in hidden costs and that lowering prices usually pressures the staffing supplier to reduce service levels. Competitive staffing firms also make it easy for customers to discuss their concerns. They train employees to listen to and address such concerns quickly and report them to management. Astute managers look for patterns of problems that can be solved or mitigated using systemic solutions instead of having to fight a lot of individual fires.

Heed warning signs from employees

Sometimes, employees give warning signs. Those warning signs may be subtle, especially when employees have a reason to fear speaking up. We describe a particularly sticky situation that occurs from time to time: highly productive managers who are reckless. While reckless managers may constitute no more than 20% of all managers, they account for more than 80% of all human resources liability and exposure in the workplace. (In reality, the ratio may be more like 10/90.)

This means that a very small proportion of management and supervisory staff (typically only one person in a smaller company) will account for the overwhelming majority of a staffing firm's:

- interpersonal conflict
- employee dissatisfaction
- employee grievances
- government agency complaints
- legal & insurance costs
- liability exposure
- senior management resources (a cost that is frequently overlooked)

These costs make it imperative that top management identify reckless managers.

It is ironic that the 10% to 20% of managers who are reckless may also be among the most productive managers. Even so, the corporate risk that they impose is certainly not worth retaining them in their reckless mode. However, their high performance potential creates a strong reason to do everything possible to try to coach, correct and, when possible, retain them.

Taming is possible, but true reform is unlikely

Coaching and strong performance management actions can be very effective, but only for managers who see a need to change. An excellent coach will provide a manager with anonymous feedback from peers, employees, and supervisors that puts a mirror to his/her bad behavior and helps the manager see the consequences of his/her behavior. The coach cajoles the manager to empathize with the people who suffer those consequences and persuades the manager that it's time to change. The manager may make a public commitment to change and practices new behaviors, then goes back to the coach to discuss the results and perhaps work on additional issues.

Reckless managers who cannot empathize with the workers whose lives they make miserable do not see why they should alter their behavior. Some of them even blame workers for being "too sensitive." When coaches and top managers hear that kind of talk from a reckless manager, it's often a sign that the person will not reform him/herself.

There are few absolute thresholds for reckless managerial behavior that automatically trigger the need for immediate termination. The rights of all parties need to be protected and balanced, but this should not be used as an excuse to retain reckless managers who engage in unacceptable behavior — especially after they have been warned.

Top managers should provide reckless managers with written warnings, although they may not be obligated to do so. And they must act if the manager's behavior doesn't change. A pattern of warnings followed by repetitive risky conduct may substantially increase the staffing firm's vulnerability to later litigation — frivolous or legitimate. It is almost always a professional human resources management/legal judgment call. Top management should ask human resources and legal experts for guidance. It is part of the challenge and responsibility of being in charge. (See chapter 1 for more on taming reckless managers.)

Avoid dysfunctional management practices

Albert Einstein reportedly described insanity as "doing the same thing over and over again and expecting different results." Yet some staffing company owners and managers — although they probably are not insane — routinely do exactly that.

Most industrial-organizational psychologists recognize the simple principle that past behavior and performance are the best predictors of future behavior and performance. This applies to employees, customers and competitors alike. But many, if not most, managers don't operate according to that principle, often out of a naïve/altruistic belief or hope that situations and people will somehow change and that they will "do the right thing." This management behavior hurts the organization because it is ineffective and dissipates resources.

There is a story about a patient who tells the doctor that it hurts whenever he lifts his right arm above his head while turning to the left. "If it hurts, don't do it," the doctor replies. Staffing managers would be well advised to heed that advice. Stop doing the same old things that are not producing the results you want.

The following examples illustrate some common problems, all of which can be solved by taking the doctor's advice.

Sales reps

The staffing industry repeatedly hire sales reps who switch jobs every six months to a year, which is (not coincidentally) about how long it takes to determine whether a new sales rep is actually productive. Careful résumé review and thorough reference checking will stop these bad apples.

These ineffectual individuals always have a story and an excuse for their failure to produce. Their common rationalization is that their failure to perform is unrelated to their capabilities and potential and is instead due to poor management, bad customers, a difficult business environment, predatory peers, poor technology, bureaucratic policies or non-competitive pricing. But we hire them anyway. Don't do it!

We allow sales representatives to continue to call on prospects that have been unproductive or unresponsive, year after year. Success stories about sales reps who finally bring in a customer after many years of effort are the exception rather than the rule. It is far more likely that sales reps will persist in burning precious months (sometimes years) of selling time and resources with prospects where they have little chance of closing. We would know that if the reps did the appropriate research and the math.

Jay remembers a giant company in California that many reps and staffing services pursued aggressively because of its high name recognition and impressive volume. The problem was (and still is) that it was impossible to make money doing business with that company due to an unfortunate combination of minimum wages, repetitive tasks, abysmal workers' comp experience, low margins, lack of conversion fees and regressive management. Yet that never stopped a slew of staffing companies from going after this money-losing business — year after year. Don't do it!

We allow sales representatives to take credit for business they had no role in landing. We certainly are not advocating that you exploit your sales staff nor create a rivalry between sales and service personnel. All things being equal, when the origin of business is in doubt, it is preferable to credit a sales rep. But it is unreasonable and often demoralizing to inside staff when we automatically credit and compensate sales reps for business that they did not solicit. It also undermines any program that utilizes objective performance metrics in order to evaluate and reward staff. Don't do it!

We continue to pay incentives to non-performing sales reps and support staff. Sometimes we feel that we owe it to them. Sometimes we feel that their lack of performance is not all their fault. Sometimes we are intimidated into paying unearned incentives as a "retention tool." But isn't performance — production of new business — their whole game? When times are good and sales are high — regardless of the reason for success — there never seems to be any ambiguity about incentives. However when sales are off, we often distribute incentives anyway. Don't do it!

We continue to squander our elite sales representatives' talent and dilute their effectiveness by sending them to "networking" meetings and events that rarely result in business.

Sales reps like to attend these events. Their pitch is compelling: "I will be drinking, dining and chatting with industry leaders and decision-makers whom I can convert into customers in a relaxed social setting." But business rarely results from these encounters. Industry leaders and decision-makers rarely attend, much less make staffing decisions there. When a real industry leader inadvertently shows up at such an event, he is probably not disposed to spend much time with your sales rep. In the unlikely event that a connection occurs, the topic of discussion will rarely be staffing.

What your sales staff may uncover at these meetings are all sorts of wonderful career opportunities — outside your firm — if you let them. Don't do it!

Customers

We go out of our way to "partner" with prospects for whom price is the primary consideration. These prospects may talk quality, service and partnership, but they make decisions based on price. They expect high quality and superior service; they just don't want to pay for it. This is hardly the kind of partnership you should extend yourself to achieve. The ultimate irony is that, even if you meet these "partners'" terms and conditions, their loyalty will last only until a lower bill rate comes along. This is truly a lose/lose proposition that neither side appears to understand. Don't do it!

We convince ourselves that unrealistic and/or unreasonable prospects will change their behavior once they become customers.

This unrealistic expectation serves to justify (more accurately, rationalize) pricing decisions and service commitments that are effectively unreasonable and therefore not profitably sustainable. Marriage and family counselors remind us of the risk of entering long-term relationships with the anticipation of changing the other party, because they know that it rarely happens. It doesn't happen in business either. Don't do it!

Competitors

We agree to back up national suppliers at their most aggressive (and perhaps unprofitable) rates.

We know that some national rate structures make no fiscal sense and must be offset by more profitable retail business to be sustainable. We also understand that even minimally profitable national business requires considerable volume to justify the effort and expense needed to service it. While it may be possible for the nationals to sustain this type of low-end/high-volume business, it can only be accomplished on the backs of secondary suppliers. It is the secondary suppliers that take much of the risk for very little of the gain. They supply their best inventory and provide superior service — and make the national suppliers look good. This is a classic win/lose proposition that the nationals understand all too well. Don't do it!

We permit a competitor's VOP program to consume a disproportionate amount of our resources and drag our best branches down to mediocrity.

This pattern is common and insidious, but it is also avoidable with some effort and planning. The first step is to recognize that VOP programs can't simply be "dropped into" existing branches with the expectation that they will somehow accommodate the additional load and a change in focus.

The best staffing operators understand that a branch's successful focus should not be permitted to deteriorate. Instead, we must create a parallel service structure and assign specific staff to fulfill the unique demands and requirements of any VOP programs to be supported. Of course, filling an occasional order for a competitor does not trigger any special needs — but allowing a VOP program to monopolize your staff and resources does. Don't do it!

The bottom line

Staffing owners and managers should avoid the tendency to leave themselves at the mercy of all the forces that seem to conspire to create dysfunctional agendas for them. Instead they have to stop doing things that don't work.

Pursuing warning signs from contingent workers

The utility of the exit interview as a human resource management best practice has been well-documented over the years. Staffing firms and their customers can use exit interviews to garner information that they might not otherwise get. Specifically, the exit interview can add value and provide essential information when an assignment ends for a contingent worker and even when they must be terminated for performance or behavioral deficiencies.

For staffing firms, exit interviews provide valuable business intelligence about customer organizations, about the health of the relationship between the customer and the staffing firm, about the job itself, and about the match between the contingent worker and the job. Using exit interviews on employees and managers who leave the staffing firm, upper management in staffing firms can gain the benefits from departing employees that customers gain from exit interviews with departing contingent workers.

For customers, a professionally conducted exit interview can provide a final opportunity to retain a valued contingent worker and ensure a positive image of the organization. The mere fact that a company elects to solicit information and feedback speaks well about its internal customer service orientation. Former workers have an extraordinary ability to shape the image of your organization in the marketplace and perhaps influence your future recruiting and sales success. It pays to make the extra effort during an exit interview to insure that the image is positive.

In many ways, contingent workers are even more likely than traditional workers to be candid and responsive within the context of an exit interview. For one thing, contingent workers are more likely to view organizations from a neutral perspective and without hidden agendas. They are also less likely to be offended or resentful when their assignments end. This outcome is usually anticipated by contingent workers and thus unlikely to influence the tone of an exit interview.

Contingent workers are also more likely to become privy to politically sensitive information, because they are widely (and correctly) perceived as being "temporary" and thus unlikely to represent a threat when mainstream traditional employees' feelings and perspectives are shared with them. Thus, they do not have to develop long-term collegial "friendships" and trusting relationships in order to gain access to information and problems that may be useful for management to learn about in exit interviews.

In many organizations today, employees never share their most essential feedback with management. And the tragedy is that most employers don't take proper advantage of the exit interview opportunity when it arises. And it arises very often! Depending on the typical turnover rate and assignment duration of contingent workers in a customer organization, management might be "exit interviewing" a random sample or a carefully selected sample of contingent workers coming off assignments. This function can be delegated to the most mature and capable HR staff, who can be trained to ask effective, probing questions and take notes that management will find useful. But they probably aren't. And often when they do, they relegate this critically important function to HR assistants or to lower levels of management, who may not even pass the information along to those who need to know. We understand that this tactic entails a lot of interviews for busy managers, but the opportunity is worth exploiting.

A more compromising consequence of allowing immediate supervisors and junior management to conduct exit interviews is that adverse or even constructive feedback that might have been relevant for that individual will not be shared precisely because the interviewer may be the target of the concern or complaints themselves. Supervisors and managers tend to be less "on guard" when dealing with contingent workers, so the feedback to senior management during an exit interview has the potential to be even more valuable in gaining perspective about the adequacy and conduct of line level managers. And the knowledge that exit interviews will be conducted even with contingent workers may encourage line managers to strive for a higher threshold of performance.

Finally, the higher the level of the manager conducting the interview, and the more that they are organizationally "removed" from the immediate manager of the worker being interviewed, the more seriously workers will take the exit interview and the more candid and helpful they are motivated to be.

Ideally, managers should solicit employee feedback on a regular basis. But in practice, political realities cause workers to hold back the most candid feedback until they leave, when they have little to lose by being candid. In fact, contingent workers are generally flattered (and surprised) to be asked about their experiences. It caters to their self-esteem and ego. Sometimes for the first time, unfortunately, someone in management has actually solicited their opinion!

Use clinical interviewing techniques

Interviews often have multiple functions and multiple agendas, such as garnering information and helping to impart the best image of the company. The process can work naturally and unobtrusively when applied to shaping the final image a departing worker has of the company, while soliciting organizational perspectives and their perceptions of the management team and operational process.

Jay had to take a course on clinical interviewing skills in order to complete an industrial-organizational psychology MBA degree. He remembers scoffing at the logic of having industrial psychologists take clinical interviewing courses taught by a clinical psychologist, no less. But it turned out that the skills acquired and the knowledge gained were quite applicable to almost any business interview setting. Perhaps that's not surprising.

The underlying theme from the professor was to listen for the hidden message beneath the spoken words. That, the course professor explained, is the real value in communication. She cautioned that important messages are rarely on the surface and you usually have to look and probe for them.

As Jay learned in the class, effective interviewing requires direction, structure and practice to do it right. And even then, some people just don't get it — so they just shouldn't do it. Not everyone can be taught effective interviewing. So while anyone can remind departing workers about the need to submit a final timesheet during a quick exit interview, not everyone can elicit accurate information about what is really going on within an organization.

In order to get beneath the surface and learn about true motives, feelings and agendas, it is necessary for the interviewer to convey a receptive, enthusiastic yet "neutral" stance during the exit interview — much as might be expected during a formal investigation of "wrong doing." The interviewer must be careful not to lead the departing workers to any conclusion or agenda. But the interviewer must also create a supportive and facilitating environment such that a reluctant worker will be more willing to provide candid feedback.

The interviewer must also be able to guide contingent workers back through structured follow-up questions that they might have missed or avoided, as well as offering sensitive probes. And all while maintaining a positive image about the firm and expressing gratitude for workers' prior service. If it was easy, anyone could do it. But everyone can't, and now you know the reason why.

Structure is also the key to facilitating almost any interview, but it is especially important in an exit interview. Most interviewers will incorporate some basic boiler-plate, perfunctory questions as part of their routine, but HR management best practice would be to provide exit interviewers with the full array of structured questions as well as probable, follow-ups to those questions, and the order in which they should be asked.

Training and simulated practice sessions help refine the interviewing skills and fine-tune the process. The ability of an interview to develop and articulate appropriate probing questions on the spot, beyond the anticipated follow-ups, is the best measure of how effectively they have mastered the interviewing techniques necessary to optimize the exit interview process.

Cautions and recommendations

There are several points of concern with regard to conducting exit interviews, things to do and not to do:

- Be alert to, and aware of, the hidden agendas — such as the possible desire to do sabotage a former more successful worker whose assignment was extended, or who became a permanent employee.
- Don't permit the exit interview to serve as a forum to "revisit" a termination decision — and perhaps inadvertently create legal liability. But don't ignore credible reports of discrimination, harassment or retaliation, either, as we discuss shortly.
- Anticipate a certain level of hostility during involuntary terminations.
- Use the "need-to-know" principle when you elect to share intelligence gathered during an exit interview. There is no point in triggering a defamation cause of action.
- Do not argue with the departing workers — no matter what they say. In fact, don't even feel obligated to immediately respond to anything that emerges in the exit interview.
- Schedule the exit interview in advance of the worker's last day of service, if at all possible, and if it is not an immediate termination for cause.
- Express appreciation for the service that they have provided while they were on assignment.
- Don't attempt to force an unwilling worker to participate in an exit interview. You probably can't, from a legal perspective, and you definitely should not. And even if you could, you certainly would not expect candid feedback.
- Make certain that if an allegation of discrimination or harassment

emerges during the exit interview, it is treated as it would be at any other point in the working process. It must be properly reported and it must trigger a timely and professionally conducted investigation, whether conducted by your organization or by your staffing supplier, or both.

- While some practitioners recommend that exit interview not be attempted with workers who are being terminated prior to the conclusion of their assignment, we disagree. There is utility to be gained by interviewing all workers before they depart. However, consideration and weighting must be given to the probable hostility that typically accompanies an involuntary termination. But that does not preclude a worker from being truthful about other work issues not related to their termination. (Be careful though!)

- Finally, it should not be assumed that all employees who are tasked with doing exit interviews really know how these can best be performed. Even professional interviewers may not understand the subtle nuances and risks associated with exit interviews. If at all possible, try to provide special training for anyone who will be conducting exit interviews for your firm.

Organizations should take advantage of one of the most effective, albeit underutilized, mechanisms to elicit in-depth feedback about management and risk management issues that might not otherwise surface, because of the anticipated political consequences. But bear in mind that simply utilizing exit interviews does not ensure that the firm or its customers will enjoy the full potential benefit that it should derive from this tactic. Consistency, training and appropriately selected management interviewers are all keys to gaining maximum advantage from the exit interview and accessing key information that current workers are usually too afraid to share.

Use Acceptable Human Resources Practices

Many staffing customers assume that their suppliers know employment law and that they engage in HR management policies and practices that are consistent with the law. Unfortunately, that is not always that case. Few senior staffing executives are lawyers. Nor do they need to be. But they do need to understand what legally acceptable personnel policies and practices are.

It is essential to understand that "generally accepted human resource management policies and practices" are not the same as the applicable employment law. Not all lawyers grasp this concept. Some persist in the expectation that all staffing suppliers and human resource management professionals have law degrees. But judges and trial courts are smart enough to understand the distinction and typically allow human resource experts to explain it to a jury, as Jay has done on dozens of occasions.

Unlike building, electrical and plumbing codes that typically can be located and easily reviewed in a single document or source, generally accepted human resource management policies and practices cannot be found in any one source or location. That is just an operating reality in human resources and in a number of other professions. It is no different from an equally unrealistic expectation that all generally accepted Western medical and surgical policies and practices can be found in a single guidebook.

It is not that acceptable policies and practices don't exist, but rather that they are not all in one location, text or journal. There are many acceptable ways to treat a cold (none particularly effective though!) and there are a number of acceptable ways to conduct an effective sexual harassment investigation, as an example. But this should not be misconstrued to mean that any way in which a sexual harassment investigation may be conducted is acceptable, from a human resource management perspective.

The science and art of HR risk management

Human resources management is a subdiscipline of industrial-organizational psychology. Over the years there has evolved a pattern of policies and practices that are consistent with good principles for selecting and managing people. While there is typically more than one acceptable way to accomplish human resource objectives, there are absolute prohibitions on discriminatory practices or consequences that adversely impact employees — based on gender, age, race, etc. — and, of course, on sexual or racial harassment and on retaliation.

HR management includes support for company strategy, processing transactions, and risk management. Highly effective human resources departments provide strategic planning facilitation, change management planning and support, talent planning and talent management systems. Human resources departments everywhere also process transactions, such as disbursing and answering questions about benefits and payroll, and scheduling employment interviews. Good human resource risk management practices are primarily designed to preclude opportunities for discrimination, harassment and retaliation. Highly effective HR departments balance these three priorities and synergize them as much as possible.

Human resource risk management has a dual constituency and dual responsibilities within organizations. It must safeguard the rights of employees and protect them from unlawful practices (discrimination, harassment and retaliation) while also protecting the organizations from the liability associated with improper policies and practices.

Generally accepted human resource management practices allow for a variety of approaches to accomplish these objectives. These may include such techniques as preventive training, vigilant monitoring, management coaching, proper postings of employee rights and complaint channels, effective employee and management manuals, prompt and effective investigations of allegations of improper conduct, user friendly complaint procedures and mechanisms, appropriate disciplinary procedures and mechanisms to preclude retaliation, among others. Some practices need to conform to specific state laws. For instance, in some states, companies must provide all supervisors and managers with sexual harassment training on a specific schedule.

Management responsibility

It is also important to note that merely having these approaches and techniques doesn't insure that they will be used effectively. That is, in large measure, a responsibility of vigilant management to insure compliance and protect employees. Staffing companies must take reasonable and proper steps to protect their employees, even when they are dispatched to their customers. However, co-employment responsibilities are complex and technical. This is an area in which consulting with an employment lawyer or a human resource professional is prudent.

The courts have long understood the critical role that human resources plays in staffing and in the management process. Human resource experts have explained appropriate personnel policies and practices to management and to juries in employment litigation matters for many decades. Jay participated in one precedent-setting case as an expert witness for the plaintiff in Dee Kotla v. Regents of the University of California. In its decision to remand the case for retrial, the Court of Appeal of the State of California incorporated a critical footnote (referred to as "Footnote 6") which follows in its entirety:

We fashion no general rule here precluding the use of human resources experts in employment cases. We are concerned solely with Dr. Finkelman's testimony that the facts in evidence were indicators of or had a tendency to show retaliation. Expert testimony on predicate issues within the expertise of a human resources expert is clearly permissible. For example, evidence showing (or negating) that an employee's discharge was grossly disproportionate to punishments meted out to similarly situated employees, or that the employer significantly deviated from its ordinary personnel procedures in the aggrieved employee's case, might well be relevant to support (or negate) an inference of retaliation. Opinion testimony on these subjects by a qualified expert on human resources management might well assist the jury in its fact finding.

In fact, the case was retried and Jay was the testifying HR expert once again. The jury awarded more than $2 million to the plaintiff (plus millions in additional legal costs), which was more than double the original verdict.

Jan Nielsen, one of the attorneys involved in the case on behalf of the plaintiff, in an article partially in response to the Appeals Court decision, wrote, "On Jan. 28, 2004, the days of industrial psychology or human resources management being characterized as 'junk science' in courtrooms abruptly ended with the California Court of Appeal's opinion, Dee Kotla v. Regents of the University of California. Now persons with such expertise formally join the ranks of recognized experts who may testify in litigation."

Implications for staffing customers

Staffing customers should have an understanding with their staffing suppliers that they each shall abide by generally accepted human resource management practices, as described previously in this chapter. Although there is an obvious need for all parties to an employment relationship to engage in good personnel practices, there is more than one way to accomplish that objective.

It is essential that the parties not inadvertently undermine each other's human resource policies and practices, thus creating potential liability for the other. Staffing customers should not assume that their staffing suppliers are, in fact, engaging in generally accepted human resource management practices. But they need to ensure that they are, in order to protect their own interests as well as those of the contingent workers assigned to customer organizations. Smart suppliers will understand and appreciate the vigilance.

What counts as discrimination?

The Equal Opportunity Employment Commission posts on its Web site some instructive warning about what discrimination includes. Here are some examples worth paying attention to:

Under Title VII, the ADA, the Equal Pay Act, the Rehabilitation Act, and the ADEA, it is illegal to discriminate in any aspect of employment, including:

- *hiring and firing;*
- *compensation, assignment, or classification of employees;*
- *transfer, promotion, layoff, or recall;*
- *job advertisements;*
- *recruitment;*
- *testing;*
- *use of company facilities;*
- *training and apprenticeship programs;*
- *fringe benefits;*
- *pay, retirement plans, and disability leave; or*
- *other terms and conditions of employment.*

Discriminatory practices under these laws also include:

- *harassment on the basis of race, color, religion, sex, national origin, disability, or age;*
- *retaliation against an individual for filing a charge of discrimination, participating in an investigation, or opposing discriminatory practices;*
- *employment decisions based on stereotypes or assumptions about the abilities, traits, or performance of individuals of a certain sex, race, age,*

religion, or ethnic group, or individuals with disabilities; and

- *denying employment opportunities to a person because of marriage to, or association with, an individual of a particular race, religion, national origin, or an individual with a disability. Title VII also prohibits discrimination because of participation in schools or places of worship associated with a particular racial, ethnic, or religious group.*

Employers are required to post notices to all employees advising them of their rights under the laws EEOC enforces and their right to be free from retaliation. Such notices must be accessible, as needed, to persons with visual or other disabilities that affect reading.

The EEOC Web site goes on to note that states have passed laws protecting employees from additional forms of discrimination. It describes in greater detail what an employer must do in a variety of situations, for instance to accommodate an employee's disabilities. It describes how charges of discrimination can be filed, within what period of time, and what processes are involved.

Staffing firms that do all the right things need not be afraid of charges. With good faith efforts and good legal counsel, they will come away from charges with minimal consequences.

Too much risk-management focus

As we mentioned previously, highly effective HR departments balance and synergize three imperatives: strategic support, transactional activities, and risk management. Top executives need their firms to be nimble in response to market changes and new strategies; and a culture of risk aversion can slow a company down dramatically. When HR departments focus too much on risk management and scare managers into inaction, they can pull a company into an unhealthy risk aversion. In the process, they alienate action-oriented executives and lose the support they need to manage risks effectively.

Risk aversion can invade a company's culture. Where risk-averse executives or HR create a risk-averse culture, the company can become mired in debilitating analysis paralysis or egalitarianism. For instance, managers may try to provide all employees with the same treatment even when situational differences warrant small changes in treatment. In extreme cases, employers fail to give special rewards or recognition to especially hard working and high-performing workers. Sameness in the name of fairness can diminish workers' motivation to excel.

In companies that are comfortable with risk, a risk-averse HR department can alienate itself and lose its ability to manage risks across the firm. Risk-averse HR departments may fall into a habit of adding extra steps to their processes, such as having managers review every specialist's work or even requiring reviews of reviews. "We have always done it this way" and "We'd better check it to be safe" become their mantras.

For instance, it may take such a department weeks to schedule interviews and process offers to new hires, while the best candidates get hired at nimbler firms. As a result, managers may go around HR and expose the company to unnecessary risk.

Executive recruiters thrive on providing services to starved hiring managers who complain that there just aren't any good candidates out there. Effective HR departments can help hiring managers use such services wisely when the department lacks the resources to find candidates who are truly needles in haystacks. But an HR department that has alienated managers cannot protect the company from unscrupulous vendors who cater to reckless managers.

While providing executive recruiting services, Jonathan turned down hiring managers' unethical requests for "All-American engineers." In the absence of a vigilant and respected HR department at the customer company, such managers would eventually find unscrupulous recruiters to take such a job order.

In one egregiously self-destructive case, Jonathan attempted to serve a company that was reportedly desperate to hire a few highly specialized engineers who were in short supply. We sent over an African engineer who had a list of impressive patents on his résumé — earned at respected U.S. firms — and extraordinarily positive references. The engineer reported seeing an executive's face fall when they first met. After a perfunctory interview, an executive claimed that the engineer lacked critical skills for the job. Perhaps even a powerful HR manager might have failed to convince racist executives that hiring a black man who could run circles around the company's white engineers was better than letting the company sink into oblivion. But with more ethical executives, strategically oriented HR managers can help executives see the synergy between ethics and success.

Protection from Underperformance and Biased Measurement Systems

Staffing firms must recruit and select talented staff and then manage their performance. How do they know which people are talented before they hire them? How do they keep tabs on employee performance? Most firms use employment tests to find the best candidates and performance appraisals to track individual performance. But improper testing can land a staffing firm in court. Firms should use tests that are reliable, fair, and valid for predicting performance on the job for which people are being hired or appraised. In the case of performance appraisal, validity means the extent to which the evaluation is a fair and accurate reflection of actual job performance and effectiveness.

Use a valid employment test or don't test at all

Ah the temptation ... a simple test or two and all your selection problems are solved. Or are they? The pitch sounds so good. "Save time, save money, save the cost of bad or incompatible hires. Your candidates can even complete the tests on the Internet." What could be more simple? Why wouldn't you want to take advantage of such a wonderful opportunity?

Before you consider testing, you must have not only a good reason but an effective, valid, non-discriminatory tool. Testing can be a very effective tool for skills assessment (you probably don't want to estimate word processing proficiency in an interview!) or general problem-solving ability, but do you really think that you can measure management proficiency or organizational "fit" with a test? It's not impossible, but it isn't easy.

Many test suppliers are legitimate and offer fine products. However, in Jay's experience as an industrial-organizational psychologist who has spent much of his professional career in the staffing industry, there are some very questionable products being marketed very effectively to the staffing industry.

Spotting a good test from a poor one: validation

An effective test is designed to reduce subjectivity and human error in selection decisions. Validation tells you the degree to which the test actually measures what it purports to measure. In her book *Psychological Testing*, eminent psychologist and psychometric expert Anne Anastasi says, "Validity provides a direct check on how well the test fulfills its function." That function is to predict performance on the specific job for which a person is being considered. Validity, in other words, isn't just about the test itself, it's about the match between what a test measures and the knowledge, skills, and abilities required for a specific job.

Without it, your testing program may look, sound and feel good but be meaningless or, worse, be a negative predictor of job performance. Yes, that really happens; higher scores on an invalid test may be inversely related to job effectiveness. You can't know without validation — up front, not afterwards.

Testing vulnerability and liability

Some of the issues associated with the use of tests that are not properly validated for their intended use are obvious; others are more subtle in their adverse effects.

- Invalid tests may "deselect" or eliminate candidates who would have been optimal for the job.
- Invalid tests may be biased against top candidates with atypical or unusual qualities that are downgraded on the test but might have made them unusually effective on the job, had they been given the opportunity.
- Invalid tests subject you to potential liability if an applicant who is not selected elects to sue for discrimination. The use of an unvalidated psychometric instrument limits your defense opportunities. If you don't clear your prospective test with an industrial-organizational psychologist, sooner or later you are likely to have to consult your employment attorney in regard to a discrimination complaint or lawsuit. You may want to discuss your potential liability with your attorney before using a test.
- The use of invalid tests is unethical because of their probable adverse

job impact on qualified candidates who should have been offered the positions.

What to avoid

There are several red flags that should prompt you to pursue further information about a vendor's validation of its tests. While the following conduct or representations may be associated with an effective and valid testing program, they raise concerns that require further investigation:

- Lack of a documented professional validation study, supplied by the test provider, that is applicable to your employment situation. (An industrial-organizational psychologist should review the documentation if you have any doubts about its adequacy and application.)
- Not being able to find documentation of the test in a known professional reference source such as the Mental Measurements Yearbooks.
- If a test provider tells you that validation is not important or that it can't be provided for review, choose another vendor.
- An offer to "custom interpret" test scores according to guidelines that cannot be defined operationally, documented or reviewed may be appropriate when a psychologist is using special tests that typically require certification by reputable publishers to administer, but it is rarely appropriate for self-administered tests. Ask what additional information (to which you are not privy) is being used to make the judgment calls.
- Hidden scoring systems that you do not understand or that may not be defensible in court should make you wary. An invalid test may use inappropriate questions to derive indefensible assessments about candidates. It is certainly possible that test items that appear to make no sense will turn out to be valid, but there is no way to determine this in advance of validation.
- An "interest inventory" is not an assessment device. Such tests may be fine for vocational counseling, but they typically are not effective predictors of job success. How can you tell the difference? Validation.

Self-administered and remotely administered tests may be convenient and "user-friendly," but they are subject to a variety of errors that you should be aware of. For example, a remotely administered test may not adequately protect you against a candidate's cheating and consulting with other parties before responding. You may not even know who is actually taking the test. We always worry about test programs where you can't actually see who is being evaluated and under what circumstances, but validation can help you make a decision about whether or not to use one of these tests.

Even when the right person is taking the test, candidates are likely to give responses that are socially desirable. Validated tests allow for and correct such "social desirability" in candidates' responses. This is a difficult and technical area to address, but there are accepted psychometric techniques that deal with social desirability when testing is used for selection purposes. An industrial-organizational psychologist can explain further, or you can simply rely on a professionally administered validation study to assure you that there is no problem.

Avoid vendors that claim that their tests will be custom validated for your firm. While this is possible (and it is even a good idea to "locally validate" any psychometric device you elect to use), such a test cannot substitute for an already validated and documented instrument. If you intend to use the test to select or deselect candidates, it simply is not acceptable or safe to use an unvalidated test. (Doing a classic "predictive validity study" might require that you hire all candidates regardless of their test scores in order to see whether the test was valid. Wouldn't you prefer to use a test that has already been validated by a provider?)

What to look for

Checking for a few specific pieces of information will help you select a valid test. Ask the vendor to provide a clear, documented statement of the test's statistical validity. Verbal assurances are not sufficient; too much is at stake. You need to see specific published confirmation of any validity claims for the test.

The validation statement should identify clearly the sample groups used in the validation studies. For example, a test that was purportedly validated in a civil service environment is not an appropriate instrument if you are looking for a staffing company manager.

Similarly, you should not use a test for outside sales representatives that was validated on college sophomores. There is no such thing as an all-purpose test.

Look for confirmation that the test complies with the non-discrimination provisions of the federal Uniform Guidelines on Employee Selection. You need to be sure that the test will not have an adverse effect on protected group members (i.e., women, applicants over 40, African-Americans or other protected groups) other than for competencies required for their actual job performance. These are tricky issues that are best left to the testing experts and lawyers.

Look for a statement of the limitations of the test to guide you in understanding its appropriate use as well as the circumstances in which it would be contraindicated. For example, a test may not have been designed for use with existing employees. Unless you are a psychometric specialist or a testing professional, it will be difficult to determine these restrictions on your own. If none are provided, that may be a warning sign.

Just because a test provider has a manual that presents validation data doesn't mean that the test is valid for predicting job performance. Jonathan served on a test review board that examined dozens of test manuals and found most of them inadequate.

In some cases, the sample groups used in the validation studies differed completely from the population taking the test. Some validation studies involved numerous small samples stitched together rather than a random sampling from the population being tested.

Some studies failed to measure important sources of unreliability. Studies measured test-retest reliability, which examines the extent to which test takers give the same responses both times they take the same test, but not the internal consistency of the items, which is a form of reliability that examines the extent of correlation between test items purporting to measure the same thing.

Finally, some validation studies examined whether sections of the test that were designed to measure different traits actually differed in the scores that they gave, but didn't examine how well each section predicted job performance.

Seek professional advice

It's not a bad idea to consult an industrial-organizational psychologist, or at least a human resources professional specifically trained in testing and measurement (be cautious — most HR managers do not have this training), about the test you are considering. If a test publisher advises you that such a verification step is unnecessary or refuses to cooperate with the process, choose another vendor.

It is also a good idea to review with an employment lawyer the risks and liabilities associated with the use of the test in the specific application that you are considering. There is no substitute for a legal review to ensure your peace of mind and warn you of any hidden risks you may not have anticipated or prepared for.

Are we being too cautious? We don't think so. Testing has enormous potential for good but there are significant risks associated with its misuse, deliberate or inadvertent. It is a mistake to count on being lucky or to assume that nothing bad will happen because it has not thus far. In addition to the issues of effectiveness, missed opportunities and ethics previously raised, you should not underestimate your liability associated with improper testing. Guide yourself accordingly.

Avoiding risk in job interviews

Job interviews can be another source of risk. Because they are such high-stakes methods for selection, academic researchers have put the lowly job interview through validation studies and found it wanting. Job interviews are notoriously poor predictors of future job performance, yet employers rely heavily on them. Too often, job interviews measure simply how much the interviewer likes the candidate.

There are ways to improve job interviews. The procedure resembles an abbreviated employment test development process. The result is a structured interview system sometimes called "behavioral interviews."

First, hiring managers or human resources professionals need to conduct a job analysis to identify the critical knowledge, skills, and attitudes that differentiate excellent performers on a specific job.

Second, an expert — preferably an industrial-organizational psychologist

— needs to design structured interview questions that elicit information that sheds light the candidate's knowledge, skills, and attitudes in each area that that job analysis found critical. The interview designer should develop two kinds of questions: forward-looking (hypothetical) behavioral questions and backward-looking ("retrospective") behavioral questions. Forward-looking questions give a scenario specific to the job for which the candidate has applied and ask the candidate what he or she would do in such a situation. Retrospective questions ask candidates to think of a time when a specific kind of situation occurred as identified in the job analysis. For instance, an interviewer might ask a management candidate, "Think of a time when you gave a performance review to a worker who was well-liked, but failing miserably on the job. Tell me what happened and why you decided to take the actions that you took."

Studies show that candidates' responses to hypothetical questions correlate more with intelligence while their responses to retrospective questions correlate more with their past track record; but both types of questions predict future performance — probably different aspects of future performance.

Third, hiring managers and other interviewers need to be trained to conduct behavioral interviews and rate candidates' responses consistently.

Assure that performance appraisal systems are valid

People don't usually consider performance appraisal systems as forms of testing, but they are. And ensuring that those systems work can be even more challenging than finding employment tests that are valid for selecting people for a specific type of job.

Staffing firms that resist implementing performance appraisal systems or fail to take them seriously, run the risk of keeping workers who lack the talent and motivation to perform. Worse, they may fail to recognize and reward workers for excellent performance and recognize poor performers, instead diminishing everyone's motivation to excel. But biased, unreliable, or invalid performance appraisal systems can be worse than no system at all.

Testing devices, including performance appraisals, are uniquely vulnerable to claims of bias and discrimination. Just because a performance appraisal system uses numbers and rankings to rate workers doesn't mean they are reliable and valid. An unreliable measurement system is analogous to someone looking at a watch that may be "off" by five or 10 minutes and confidently announcing the "exact" time — to the second. The process of incorporating apparent numerical precision within a measure is typically misconstrued as a sign of the accuracy of the measure — be it the time of day or a performance rating. When most employees and managers hear numbers and fractions associated with a performance evaluation, they are inclined to attribute greater rigor and accuracy to that measure. Unfortunately, that confidence may be misguided.

Vulnerability and risk

Typical performance appraisal programs in staffing firms are almost as vulnerable to charges of bias and discrimination as the deservedly maligned job interview. While these charges may be difficult to demonstrate and sustain, the quantification attributes that make performance appraisals so compelling can also be used to document inconsistencies that may be interpreted as discrimination.

The perception of discrimination in employment, while always unfortunate, is particularly destructive when it is held by employees who are disgruntled but remain with the company. Unlike job applicants who are not hired or employees who have been terminated, active employees who believe that they have been subject to bias in their job evaluations may seethe unproductively in their positions before ultimately consulting an attorney. Obviously, this is highly counterproductive to the intended objective of performance appraisal systems, which is to enhance job performance.

A legal challenge is even more likely if a poor performance review results in an adverse job action such as a demotion or salary reduction. Does this suggest that performance appraisal programs should not be used to support or initiate adverse job action? Absolutely not — unless your only management objective is to avoid potential litigation. This truly would be allowing the tail to wag the dog!

Properly administered and monitored performance appraisal programs help companies evaluate the utility and appropriateness of their human resource decisions — including adverse job actions. The key operative words are "properly administered and monitored."

Ensure ratings consistency to reduce risk

Most staffing firms lack the resources or the motivation to establish or defend the validity and reliability of their performance appraisal programs. But the issue of validity is not a firm's greatest potential vulnerability. Lack of consistency in performance evaluation presents a greater risk.

The good news is that appraisal consistency is attainable if you train your managers to focus on that objective and continuously monitor the program.

It is essential to ensure that adverse employment actions are not contradicted by adequate or even positive performance evaluations and that the language (including praise) used in performance evaluations is consistent with subsequent employment actions. There is nothing more awkward, or less defensible, than giving an employee a positive review followed by a negative job action. Make sure that you don't have to defend yourself in that scenario.

Plaintiffs' lawyers and employment experts look for patterns and inconsistencies. Staffing company management should do the same thing and act aggressively to correct any indefensible relationships between job ratings and job actions. Often the inconsistencies are motivated by managers' sincere desire to please and flatter their employees or simply to be liked by them.

Regardless of the nature of the motivation, anything that generates inconsistencies between job ratings and actual performance is dangerous, counterproductive and an obvious abdication of management responsibility. In addition to undermining the integrity of an effective performance appraisal program, such inconsistencies will rarely be excused in a lawsuit.

Each of the following sequences presents a high level of risk due to inconsistencies:

1. Consistent satisfactory performance ratings followed by adverse job action. The inconsistency here between ratings and the job action is obvious.

2. A pattern of satisfactory performance ratings followed by a single unsatisfactory rating followed by an adverse job action. In this case, the deviation from the original satisfactory rating pattern followed by an adverse job action may appear to be a set-up or even retaliation.

3. Consistent unsatisfactory performance ratings over an extended period of time, finally followed by an adverse job action. Management's failure to take action in the face of a long and consistent pattern of unsatisfactory ratings undermines the accuracy and integrity of the ratings and also suggests the possibility of retaliation.

Get buy-in for the performance appraisal system

There is nothing like forcing managers to determine raises and promotions using a performance measurement system that doesn't make sense to them. Performance appraisals are a high-anxiety experience for managers and workers alike. When managers don't believe in the system, workers can feel it. Word gets around that the system is nonsensical, and the grapevine circulates stories to back up that notion.

So far, we have discussed technical excellence in performance appraisal systems. But technical excellence is not enough. The most effective performance appraisal systems begin with human resources experts meeting with managers and workers to build the system together. Such a performance appraisal system development task force includes technical experts, and managers and workers from around the firm. The experts take the time to explain the technical principles for achieving reliability and consistency, validity, and fairness. Managers and workers contribute to the language and layout of performance appraisal worksheets, the wording and structure of performance review conversations, the methods for recognizing high performers, and the training systems. Because designing and implementing an effective performance appraisal system may involve killing a few sacred cows, the task force should be led by a politically astute leader and include representatives from groups that could torpedo a new system.

Before implementing them, the task force selects several managers to pilot the new system to work out the bugs. Next, they train the managers how to conduct effective performance appraisal discussions. Then, they gather evaluation data to determine how well each element of the system works. Finally, they tweak the system based on the feedback. And, so long as the pilot gives a green light, executives and the task force members market the new system to managers and workers until everyone buys in.

Once the performance appraisal system is in place, executives and HR listen for feedback from workers and managers to make sure that the system makes sense to people and has broad-based support. Astute professionals realize that workers and managers will naturally complain about a high-stakes, anxiety producing process such as performance appraisal and take the complaints in stride. Most important, they distinguish from anxiety-based complaints and red flags that signal a technical problem such as inconsistent ratings or a lack of political support from an important constituency.

The bottom line

Professional, monitored performance appraisal programs have great utility for staffing firms, but specific precautions and guidelines must be followed to maximize their benefit and minimize risk:

- Use a validated appraisal tool. Remember that timing is (almost) everything when job performance ratings are compared with subsequent job actions.
- Never allow adverse job actions to be taken that are inconsistent with the employee's performance appraisal ratings and/or management's comments and documentation.
- Never accept "satisfactory" ratings for unsatisfactory performance.
- Whenever possible, require empirical documentation for subjective job performance ratings.
- Utilize one-over-one management sign-offs on performance reviews.
- Ensure buy-in from executives, managers, workers, and HR experts by using a broad-based task force to develop or review the performance appraisal system.
- Finally, ensure that a trained human resources professional monitors the program. The goal is not only avoiding adverse legal action by employees but enhancement of their loyalty to and performance for the company.

Seek Support from Trusted Advisors

Trusted advisors, especially attorneys, accountants, bankers, and industrial-organizational psychologists, can help staffing managers reduce risk by sorting out complicated issues. We discussed some specific examples in the sections on management responsibility, testing, and performance appraisal systems. Several legal issues warrant support from outside sources. In this section, we discuss three important sources: legal templates available from industry associations, an attorney's advice and editing of critical documents, and a strong governance system at the top – especially an ethical and proactive board of directors. We also focus on indemnification agreements, as they are an important issue for many staffing firms.

Templates for legal documents

In most situations, branch or area managers should rely on the staffing firm owner or executive management in larger companies to provide the necessary legal forms and phrases for running the business. These include timecard language, sales contracts, direct-to-hire and guarantee terms, and government-required employment forms. In turn, the staffing firm owner would do well to invest in legal advice regarding the same.

Membership in an association such as the American Staffing Association (ASA) or the National Association of Computer Consultant Businesses (NACCB) will give access to model agreements, timecards, templates, and other useful marketing and operating materials. State-level chapters of these organizations offer local opportunities to network with other owners and managers who may offer advice.

Formal networks of small to midsize firms can provide industry-specific support to their members. There are a number of groups of staffing firms that meet periodically during the year to exchange expertise and experiences, and offer training to individual staffers. At least a couple of them have more than 100 members across the country, but most are smaller. The key to building trust among the firms in each network is that they don't compete for customers in the same geographic areas.

Indemnification agreements

No risk management discussion would be complete without addressing an increasingly common demand being made by many staffing customers today. It is the requirement that suppliers sign an "indemnification" clause – sometimes also referred to as a "hold harmless" agreement. It is our perspective that this is a particularly insidious and unfair imposition by larger customers that use their considerable leverage to the detriment of staffing suppliers. The precise language is typically supplied by counsel for the customer. It attempts to shift the liability burden as much as possible from the customer — the end user of the contingent workers — to the staffing supplier.

We characterize it as unfair because customers are essentially the sole beneficiaries of the services of the contingent workers whom you are supplying, and they usually have the primary responsibility to orient, train, and supervise the workers. So what is the rationale for asking staffing suppliers to assume that responsibility? None, really, other than the fact that they can. And in the words of Michael Douglas (as Gordon Gekko) in the movie *Wall Street* — "Greed is good!" But obviously not for staffing suppliers.

Unfortunately, most staffing suppliers feel obligated to yield to the pressure (and the anticipated rewards) of signing agreements that they know are risky and imprudent. Customers take advantage of this knowledge because they know that other staffing firms will always be willing if their first choice declines. Therefore, few firms actually decline to sign.

It may be worth it to try to negotiate less onerous language with the aid of your attorney. But don't anticipate great receptivity to the prospect from most customers, especially the largest customers. They understand their clout within the staffing industry. A Fortune 100 company that did more than $100 million in contingent staffing business once explained to Jay that even though it really wanted his staffing organization as a "partner," it was a deal-breaker if his staffing firm didn't sign. The staffing firm attorneys reviewed the document, reported that it was outrageous, yet the staffing firm signed it anyway!

Having said this, the risk of signing indemnification-type agreements is so great, in a worst case scenario, that it is essential to have counsel review any such agreement to explain the level of exposure to top management, before making a business decision to take the risk. Perhaps if more firms were willing to hold their ground in these one-sided negotiations, supplying large customers would become less risky for staffing firms.

Good governance, especially at the board of directors level

A proactive and engaged board of directors can provide extraordinary value to staffing firms, both public and private. However, the value is probably greatest to smaller staffing companies as they embark on their growth and expansion plans. Larger firms typically have the internal sophistication to provide proper guidance to senior management and owners.

However, internal politics have a way of distorting the information that employees provide to managers and managers provide to executives, especially if it is perceived to be inconsistent with the direction being set by the top decision makers. Hence, the utility of a truly independent board that is not fearful of the reaction of owners or executives to their candid opinions and cautions. Of course, some supposedly independent boards are shams, appointed by owners and presidents essentially to support and "rubber stamp" their decisions. Unfortunately this occurs all too often in our industry.

There is a dysfunctional "reciprocity" in which board members are appointed, compensated, and treated to exotic management retreats in return for their "permission" to approve what executives want to do, regardless of whether it is prudent. Friends and families of owners of small and regional firms are notorious for this practice. Thus an important source of guidance, control, and innovation is lost to the organization. In contrast, a competent and empowered board of directors can direct executives away from potential disasters and truly catapult a staffing firm to new levels of greatness.

Risk management issues are rarely exciting or inspirational for staffing managers, but they are critical. The trick is to not to ignore them and not to let them drive your business practices. Compliance can be achieved without sacrificing competitiveness, entrepreneurship and innovation. Highly competitive staffing firms have learned that some of the best practices designed to mitigate risk are also best practices from a pure business perspective, as well. For example, what is the point of using an invalid and discriminatory selection test that can't identify the best workers? In contrast, best practices, as described in this chapter, are safe because they work and they work because they are safe!

Chapter Seven

MANAGING STAFFING FIRM PROFITABILITY

Highly competitive staffing firms maximize their profits by satisfying their customers, internal staff, and contingent workers while maintaining their efficiency. Profitability results from combining competence in the first six areas we have already discussed in this book with a set of financial and structural rules and practices that are industry-specific and critical to the staffing services business.

First, we examine the bottom line: what it is and what drives it. Next, we discuss key principles for managing growth profitably in the staffing industry, including cash management principles, pools of funding specific to the staffing industry and principles for balancing growth with the firm's leadership and financial capacity.

Finally, we look at how non-core processes can be designed, supported by vendors, or even outsourced entirely to improve profitability, and some of the pitfalls involved in each.

In this chapter we focus on a range of processes, decisions, and relationships where managers and owners can affect their branch or firm profitability. Specifically, we cover:

- Driving the Bottom Line through Metrics
- Managing Growth Profitably
- Designing and Outsourcing Non-core Processes
- Orchestrating Business Growth

Driving the Bottom Line through Metrics

Financial and operational analysis do not come easily to most staffing managers. They are typically "people people." They are more comfortable meeting and greeting than doing the systematic review of past company data that is necessary to understand how a business is likely to perform going forward. But such analysis is usually essential for operating a profitable business. It requires systematically reviewing historical records of firm and branch performance in order to understand what is working and what could be improved in operations.

Management experts like to say, "You can't expect what you can't inspect." Without the ability to measure, there's no yardstick for gauging progress or success. (For more on this, see the section on SMART goals in chapter 1.) Understanding the important metrics for the staffing industry — and using them effectively to manage and build the business — is certainly a key factor in staffing profitability; failing to keep an eye on the numbers that measure the health of critical operations in a staffing firm would leave any manager floundering.

The first step is to determine what to measure regarding the firm's business activities and the results of those activities. Then, the staffing firm must consistently collect those data. Highly competitive staffing firms measure all core processes and outcomes that matter to the firm and to its customers. They also benchmark their numbers against industry averages, expecting much better results in areas that represent their firm's specific competitive advantages and calibrating their expectations based on the firm's business mix, customer needs, and regional differences.

One recent innovation offered by Staffing Industry Analysts (SIA) enables a staffing firm to compare its metrics with a set of industry benchmarks on a quarterly basis. SIA's "Staffing Industry Benchmark Consortium" enables managers to see how they compare to firms of similar size, location, and sector specialty.

The most useful metrics for staffing managers have not changed dramatically over the years, although the tools for measuring them have become more sophisticated and numerous. Available industry-specific software or ASP suites can calculate a wide variety of useful metrics — provided the staffing firm inputs the necessary data! The 'garbage in-garbage out' rule still applies in data processing: input must be consistent, accurate, timely, relevant and complete if you expect to get useful metrics as output. (See chapter 5, Exploiting Technology, for more details.)

Good financial and operational metrics support success in sales and in designing a rational reward structure. In the following sections we discuss metrics for operational analysis and financial analysis. For some readers, the technical details will be a breezy refresher; for others, it will be a learning experience. We start with operational metrics because they will be familiar to managers at all levels. We go into greater detail on financial metrics because they are more comparable across firms and because some readers will need to be filled in on the basics.

Measuring the bottom line

Financial analysis focuses on the bottom line and on the results of the firm's sales and operations that most directly drive the bottom line.

Successful staffing management reviews not only overall firm performance, but also which parts of the business are profitable and which parts are not. They can use cost and revenue data to determine which contracts, types of business, sales activities, and recruiting sources will have the most profit potential, and which will have the least.

The bottom line can be measured in many ways, and accounting experts can go into great detail on the merits of looking at gross margins versus operating profit and debt ratios. Here, we focus on a few basic concepts of which all managers should be aware.

Sales results and immediate drivers of the bottom line can be measured with such metrics as orders received per week, orders per salesperson or branch, orders filled, orders completed, new customers, new recruits, paycheck errors, etc. Successful staffing managers want to know how new accounts and new recruits were obtained, and by whom.

Gross margin

The difference between the bill rate for contingent workers and the direct costs of employment (defined as pay rate plus mandatory benefits such as workers' compensation, unemployment insurance, employer's share of FICA, state or local taxes, plus optional benefits) is considered to be the "gross margin" for a contingent worker on assignment in the United States. A company's total gross margin is the difference between its total billings and its total direct employee costs.

The average gross margin for 10 selected large U.S. public staffing companies in 2008 was 25.8%, but there has been a high rate of variance. In 2008, Robert Half International was at the high end for these public staffing providers with gross margin of 40.7%, while Kelly Services Inc. and Manpower Inc. were at the low end (17.7% and 18.4%, respectively).

In the case of Robert Half, its very high margins come from a combination of higher professional bill rates in some business units, higher retail markups in others, longer assignments (which reduce SG&A costs), plus a robust search business in the accounting and financial sectors that serves to elevate the overall margin percentage and drops real profit right to the bottom line.

Gross margins at U.S. staffing companies may vary considerably by type of skill provided, volume of business, local demand for talent, length of assignment, and the extent of permanent placement or search business conducted. Pure margins on contingent workers may also vary significantly, all the way from below 10% to well in excess of 30%. Typically, contingent worker margins fall in the range of 15% to 25%, depending on the service line and size of account.

Comparative margins

While knowing the overall gross margin for the industry is interesting, having benchmarks that are more directly comparable for firms in similar business segments provides a better measure of relative performance. Operating conditions vary widely across segments, as does the outlook for sales growth. But the most important variations between staffing segments are in gross margin percentages as well as pay and bill rates.

In the first half of 2009, clinical staffing had gross margins at the high end of the spectrum, averaging about 28.1%. At the low end was engineering/design, with 15.3%. This variation of about 13 percentage points can make a huge difference in the economics of a staffing firm. In healthcare, the segment with the highest gross margin percentage was *locum tenens* (temporary placement of physicians) with 27.3%.

There are many reasons behind the high variability in margins by segment. Typically, this is related to the skill level being provided and the difficulty of recruiting, although not always. Certainly margins improve in areas with big shortages of workers and tend to compress as workers become more plentiful. As evidence for this, survey data from Staffing Industry Analysts have shown big declines in nursing gross margins over the years during which the nurse shortage eased temporarily.

Industrial business is typically done at margin percentages well below the average (primarily because of the higher volume per customer and a more fungible job pool), while niche providers of highly skilled professionals generally command margins well above average. In 2007, companies with more commercial staffing exposure typically had margins in the range of 18% to 19%, while their professional counterparts reported margins of 19% to 28%, according to data from Staffing Industry Analysts.

No staffing segment delivers higher margins than the *locum tenens* segment of healthcare staffing. With an average gross margin percentage of 27.3% and an average bill rate of nearly $150 per hour (in 2009 dollars), this segment appears to be quite lucrative. Of course, anyone involved in serving the physician staffing market will mention that the high gross margin dollars go to cover very high malpractice insurance costs and that the overall volume of *locum tenens* is quite small. This is a true niche business, requiring highly specialized skills and providing premium margins for those who succeed.

Computing operating profit

The higher a staffing firm's gross margin, the more cash that will be left over to cover all other SG&A costs (salaries, commissions, rent, equipment, services, etc.) and provide profit to owners. Typically, competitive staffing firms carry only 2% to 6% of revenue to the bottom line pre-tax, and require in the neighborhood of 18% to 21% for total SG&A expenses (sometimes called "operating costs"). Specialty niche firms can sometimes generate as much as 10% to 15% in pre-tax profit, but those are few and far between in the staffing industry.

All too often, failure in staffing firm management stems from a fixation with increasing revenue rather than attention to sufficient gross margin to cover other expenses and leave some profit in the business. In fact, many staffing firms have grown revenue only to see falling gross margin percentages leave them with the same or fewer gross margin dollars to spend on expenses. For those firms it's like walking the wrong way on an escalator — you have to keep moving quickly just to stay in place.

Tight cost controls are the rule and staffing firms are learning to cope with lean gross margins. Included in operating costs are all costs related to running a staffing business, other than direct costs for contingent workers such as payroll, taxes and insurance, which are included in gross margin. Also excluded from operating costs are those that are "below the line," such as interest and taxes, as well as non-cash costs such as depreciation and amortization.

Lean Profits in the Billed Hour

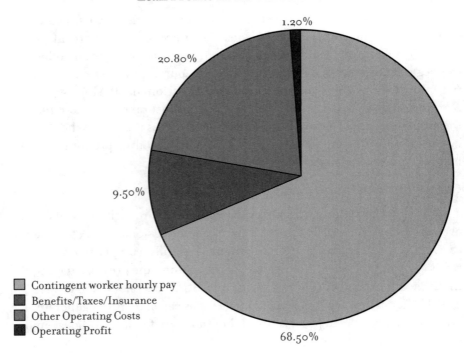

- Contingent worker hourly pay
- Benefits/Taxes/Insurance
- Other Operating Costs
- Operating Profit

Source: Staffing Industry Analysts

According to Staffing Industry Analysts, the costs associated with employing a contingent worker have shifted marginally over the years. As is shown in this chart, operating profits were slim to none in the first half of 2009, as only 1.2% of the average billed hour went to profit.

Defining markup

In a retail store, the price of an item is determined by taking its cost, and then "marking it up" to a higher price that consumers pay, which covers overhead and hopefully leaves a profit. The big concern then becomes inventory — not turning over product fast enough to pay the bills. If inventory stays too high, the cash situation deteriorates, and the result is often a "Super Blowout Sale," and almost always a greater time delay before vendor invoices are paid. A typical markup in retail might be 100% (double the cost of an item).

Calculating Markup, Margin and Operating Profit

If a contingent worker is paid $15.00 per hour, a 50% markup would produce a bill rate of $22.50. A 30% markup would require a bill rate of $19.50, and a 70% markup would require a bill rate of $25.50. So depending on the markup percentage, the identical pay rate will produce dollar markups (sometimes called the "spread") of $4.50 (at 30%), $7.50 (at 50%), or $10.50 (at 70%) per hour. Because the pay rate in this example always remains at $15.00, the higher the markup obtained, the greater the dollar spread between pay rate and bill rate, and the greater the potential profit margin. The lower the markup, the less will remain for profit after SG&A costs are subtracted.

Assuming that operating costs are about 20% of bill rates, and an employee burden (taxes and insurance) of 10% of bill rate, the total costs associated with this hour of work at a 30% markup ($19.50 bill rate) are $15.00 (pay rate), $1.95 (burden), and $3.90 (for SG&A), for a total cost of $20.85. When subtracted from the $19.50 bill rate, this produces an operating loss of $1.35. At a 50% markup, the same exercise would produce a .75 cents operating profit (or 3.3%), and at a 70% markup the operating profit per hour would be $2.65 (or 10.4%).

In the staffing industry, however, the object is to keep and grow — not sell — the inventory. The goal is to retain good contingent workers by paying them on time and keeping them working at good assignments. Pay rates (cost per hour) are marked up to generate bill rates (price per hour). Markup in the staffing industry is simply the difference between the pay rate and the bill rate, and is often expressed as a percentage of the pay rate. A typical staffing industry markup might be around 55%, but it can vary greatly from one business to the next. Customers and contingent workers often mistakenly believe markup to be all profit, but the accompanying boxed text puts that notion to rest.

Understanding SG&A costs

Costs that are not directly tied to revenue are sales, general and administrative (SG&A) expenses. These functions are as necessary as payroll to the success of your business, but the timing and extent of these expenses is somewhat discretionary. Unlike contingent worker pay and its immediate burden, which must be paid weekly (or twice a month), SG&A costs are tied less directly to levels of business. While some of these indirect costs are fixed (such as rent), other costs are variable (ads on a job board, for example). Sales costs and recruiting costs are included in SG&A, as are all inside personnel costs related to the business unit.

In times of financial stress, it is most important to look carefully and quickly at the variable costs to see what can be scaled back, halted, or postponed. Sometimes even fixed costs can be reduced as well, through the sublet of a branch office, for example. Some cost reductions — such as closing branches or decreasing the headcount of people working in critical processes or in customer-facing positions — can have serious negative effects on your future business. Competitive staffing firms take into account both the need to make cuts in spending and the need to retain some capacity to take advantage of the inevitable business upturn. As mentioned in Chapter 1, Leading People, competitive staffing firms sometimes use business downturns to let go of mediocre performers and pick up highly talented staff whose skills will add to the firm's competitive advantage when the economy turns around.

Drivers of the bottom line

Achieving higher order fill rates, reduced time to fill, a larger skilled inventory, more assignment completions, increased hours per week, and greater levels of customer satisfaction are all important drivers of staffing productivity and profitability. Staffing firms can keep customers abreast of key metrics that matter to them and work for good scores compared to industry benchmarks. For instance, the level of employee turnover prior to assignment completion affects customer productivity, especially when the assignment requires on-the-job training. Employee extension, or the number of conversions to regular employment, may also be seen as pluses by customers. And of course punctuality and absenteeism are worth tracking.

In the back-office area, billing accuracy and prompt invoicing may be major customer concerns. Both can be tracked by counting errors and days to bill. Compliance with the contract rate structure and problem response time are other measurable metrics that reflect on the operations level of branch or on-site personnel. Managers can also set goals for how productive each recruiting source should be, relative to its cost. These goals can be set specifically for any customer or VOP program.

Sophisticated firms also recognize that their own employees' perceptions are a great source of operational measurement. They measure employee satisfaction, the drivers that shape that satisfaction, and the results of that satisfaction. Employees' perceptions can illuminate how well managers lead and shape the culture of the organization. Employee survey data on various dimensions of leadership effectiveness, resource levels, process efficiency, technology support, organizational culture, employee engagement, employee commitment and intent to stay can shed light on the drivers of success in the operational measures.

Firms with even more sophisticated analytical resources can analyze operational outcomes and potential drivers to see which have the largest impact. For instance, which employee survey variables mentioned in the previous paragraph have the largest impact on employees' intent to stay? Which methods of sourcing and screening contingent workers have the best track record for predicting contingent worker outcomes, such as absenteeism, turnover prior to assignment, and extension of assignments? Or how much impact does training supplied by the staffing firm have on contingent office staff outcomes?

Competitive staffing firms focus on metrics that measure success of all critical staffing operations, drivers of customer satisfaction, and strategy implementation. Not all staffing firms are alike. Regional economic and competitive factors as well as the staffing firm's specific business model and business mix also affect which metrics to focus on and what levels the firm should try to achieve. For instance, absenteeism levels expected in light manufacturing may be higher and time-to-fill lower than for highly trained professionals in critical roles. Also, a firm that specializes in supplying hard-to-find, highly trained professional staff may focus less on time-to-fill and more on contingent worker satisfaction with the recruiting process and customer satisfaction with quality of fit.

Best practices: sales management

Selling is hard work, so we pay commissions and bonuses to motivate account managers. Recruiting, matching and managing a contingent worker workforce can be equally as challenging as selling the business, so often inside staff are also rewarded with bonuses or commissions. An effective system for commissions and bonuses can increase a firm's profitability, and we provide some principles for making it effective. Simplicity, transparency, and focus are key.

Keep it simple and transparent

Such compensation systems can be idiosyncratic and tricky. Their effectiveness is difficult to measure. And to make matters worse, certain incentive and commission programs have the potential for creating dysfunctional consequences, especially if they are administered improperly or without finesse. And this leads us to the first rule of an effective sales incentive and compensation system: keep it simple.

We have seen the most elegant and sophisticated sales incentive systems fail because only the owner or manager understood how they worked and knew they were fair. "Trust me" just doesn't cut it for most sales representatives in today's scandal-ridden business and political environments. People must understand how they are being compensated and rewarded for good performance. Otherwise, they may conclude that they are being cheated, and their performance will suffer, or they may be motivated to sabotage the system.

Cut to the chase

There is no question that most sales representatives, and certainly sales managers, quickly determine how they are really compensated and how they can maximize their income. It is human nature and there is no point in fighting it. Rather, it can be used to the advantage of the organization by making the compensation system as "transparent" as possible and have it focused on the key productivity and performance measures that you wish to influence.

If you recall the compelling portion of *Jurassic Park* in which the most aggressive dinosaurs continuously "tested" the electrified fence, probing for weaknesses and vulnerabilities, that is precisely how aggressive and successful sales representatives game the incentive systems that are in place. If there are deficiencies or compromises that may serve to their advantage, they will quickly discover them and exploit them. Why shouldn't they?

It is part of the system in which they must work and survive. Jay proudly admits to doing the very same thing when he was a sales executive. It was key to being successful. Not surprisingly, colleagues who didn't figure it out also didn't survive. At some level, it was a measure of sales savvy, if not simply basic intelligence. If this is sounding too Machiavellian, it is reality, and it must be dealt with, if not actually exploited, by successful sales organizations. And most organizations today have become sales organizations of one type or another, including virtually the entire staffing industry.

Focus sales reps on selling

There is no element of the staffing business that requires more focus than the sales function. Martial artists emphasize the importance of focus in accomplishing difficult feats that might otherwise seem impossible to the uninitiated. Breaking boards is not as difficult as it might seem, if you have the correct technique — and focus. Let us now translate this into staffing parameters.

If you place a sales representative in a split role of having to sell contingent staffing and then service what they sell, they will (almost) inevitably gravitate to the servicing side and spend less and less of their time developing new business. The issue will become especially acute as business eventually builds and servicing requirements become more onerous. New sales typically plateau and eventually decline.

It is really not fair, and it is almost always counterproductive, to place staffing firm employees in this type of situation. Rather, it is far preferable to bifurcate the sales and service functions such that a single individual (or group) is uniquely responsible for just one type of task. This avoids confusion and precludes using myriad other service-related responsibilities as an excuse for a lack of new business development activities and results. (For more details, see the section in Chapter 3 called "Keep sales and service separate.")

Assign authority and responsibility to the same person

From a human resources management perspective, it is preferable to be able to assign authority and responsibility to the same individual. But this requires that their tasks be clearly defined and as discrete as possible. Managers don't want to place employees in a position of not knowing exactly for what they will be held accountable. And they want to be able to hold employees accountable for their own performance, whether it be sales or service. But not both. It just doesn't work.

That is why we advocate complete separation of the sales and service functions within staffing firms. That separation should remain intact as high as possible through the organizational chart. Otherwise, you run the risk of undermining the effectiveness and the focus of the initial separation. Sometimes it takes courage to push reluctant sales representatives into the field to solicit new business, when they are concerned about whether their current orders will be filled properly. But it has to be done or new business development will grind to a halt. (See chapter 3, Providing Services, for a full treatment of this issue.)

It does not end there. Sales representatives must be made to focus on new business development once they are finally out of the office. It is always easier to visit and "service" existing customers, and to take them to lunch. The most successful staffing organizations have developed processes to gradually turn over responsibility for servicing existing customers to service, not sales, representatives. Typically these are "inside" representatives who are tasked with visiting and developing rapport with the existing customer base, with the initial support and mentoring of the "outside" sales representatives.

Some firms also provide financial incentives to their sales representatives in order to facilitate the account turnover process and insure its success. A best practice is to reward both sales and service representatives so as to encourage the expansion of business within existing customers. This can be tricky, however, and the process needs to be carefully managed. Training and performance feedback are particularly important tools here.

Support compensation with "high-value" HR practices

There is a trend among behavioral scientists and human resources professionals to view compensation as only a single element in supporting worker motivation and effective performance. There is no disputing the fact that performance is influenced by more than mere money. And there is some evidence that high-value practices such as ongoing training, open communication, and participative management practices make compensation systems more effective.

And then there is the unique situation of sales management. Sales is unlike any other job family. It has its own rules and practices. That is not to suggest that good human resource management practices do not have a role in any job function. Of course they do.

But for sales professionals, somehow, money seems to dominate everything. Sales representatives appreciate recognition, good leadership, effective communication and useful skills training. But most of all, they appreciate being able to earn money that ties directly to their performance — if they are, in fact, performing.

Indeed, a significant 2006 study by Lopez, Hopkins and Raymond, published in the *Journal of Personal Selling & Sales Management*, examined salespeople's preferences for commissions versus other rewards. The results of their study "support the importance of increases in commissions as a reward for salespeople across different industries and different demographic profiles. Higher commission rates were the most preferred reward, followed by pay raises." This study certainly doesn't leave much doubt about the important of commissions in motivating sales professionals.

Compensate for performance

The most confident sales professionals actually prefer lower base salaries coupled with higher commission potential. Less confident sales representatives tend to prefer the security of a higher base salary. Unfortunately, higher base salaries tend to be correlated with complacency and non-performance, especially in the staffing industry. We have successfully used this distinction as the basis for screening questions prior to recommending that customers hire sales candidates. Now, confidence in and of itself doesn't necessarily equate with long-term success, so hiring managers should not look only at that one factor when making hiring decisions.

We have also heard from excellent sales reps with families and enough years of experience to have been through an economic slowdown who prefer midlevel base salaries rather than low ones. Unfortunately, this usually means smaller bonuses, but some seasoned sales reps are willing to make that tradeoff.

The most successful entrepreneurs with whom we have consulted in the staffing industry provide a modest initial base salary for three to six months and allow it to decline after that. The presumption is that the resulting compensation gap will be more than offset by increasing commissions from sales, for high-performing sales representatives. And the presumption is also that poor performers will begin to exit on their own, as their total compensation diminishes.

The situation becomes as close to self-correcting as you can engineer in sales management. Thus, you don't have to tell unsuccessful sales personnel that they are underperforming; they know it and they feel it in their paychecks. There is no ambiguity as to whether someone is doing well or not.

Hire and train for excellence

Compensating for performance does not relieve sales management of the obligation to hire excellent sales staff and properly coach and supervise new, and even seasoned, sales representatives. For example, Jay found that new employees invariably swing for the "home runs" and don't grasp the concept of a business mix or of a prospect mix.

Thus, it is often difficult to gauge the sales proficiency of a new representative by viewing sales revenue exclusively during the first three to six months, especially if the representative is focused on landing larger target accounts and VOPs — thus, the utility of accompanying representatives, unannounced, on a number of sales calls to prospective customers. There is also a benefit in understanding the sales development process that they are using and observing early morning or late afternoon preparation. This process should not be left to chance, but rather should be the focus of ongoing training and supervision.

Keeping in mind how long it takes to determine the actual effectiveness of a sales representative in the staffing industry, managers should be very cautious about hiring "serial failures" — those who have not lasted more than six months to 18 months at any prior sales position within the industry. Amazingly, this is still the norm at many firms. Managers think they are hiring inexpensive, high-energy professionals who will inevitably have a story as to why they "elected" to leave their last two or three staffing positions.

The most popular excuses are that their previous employer(s):

- failed to pay earned commissions in a timely fashion,
- were experiencing financial difficulty and might not meet payrolls,
- did not adequately support sales with good service and fulfillment,
- engaged in unethical or discriminatory sales practices, or
- abused or harassed their sales representatives.

While any of these explanations may be credible in certain circumstances, they become increasingly improbable when they occur in rapid succession to the same sales representative, and should be viewed with some skepticism. Comprehensive reference, background and credit checks are always a good idea, with the candidate's permission.

Align sales compensation with company goals

Unfortunately, there are too many variables that are involved in determining the precise basis for an incentive compensation system for staffing sales representatives to be able to present a generic model that will be applicable across all firms, service lines, and competitive environments. In various circumstances, it may be reasonable to incorporate metrics for gross sales, gross margin dollars, net profit and even the number of VOPs that are acquired. One guiding rule for any bonus and commission structure is that it must reinforce your company's sales and profit objectives. Incentive programs must promote branch activities and results which directly enhance the company's business goals.

Why Fast Growth Can Be Dangerous

Ironically, the better your business gets, the greater your cash flow challenge can become. Let's say you employ 20 contingent workers at $20.00 per hour (including taxes), generating $12,000 in payroll costs (assuming an average workweek of 30 hours per worker). After four weeks of business, you've paid out $48,000, and billed those hours to your customers. Assuming that you collect these accounts on average in 25 days, a $48,000 line of credit would be sufficient to cover the time from paycheck distribution to remittance.

But if your business is growing by 4 contingent workers each week, you will actually need $14,400 the second week, $16,800 the third week, and $19,200 the fourth week in business. The amount coming in from your customers will always be less than the amount going out. And the faster your office is growing, the more bridge payroll financing you will need!

Ideally, customers pay within 15 to 30 days, but larger companies often take longer — as many as 60 days, and in the medical staffing segment, 60 to 90 days is all too common. The longer the customer takes to pay, the more bridge funding is needed to stay afloat.

Remember that smart sales professionals will probe for weaknesses in your incentive system and will quickly determine and exploit the true basis for their compensation. There should always be "thresholds" or sliding incentive payout scales, such that representatives are not rewarded for putting together deals that only make them money while creating net losses for the firm. We have more than occasionally seen instances in which it took firms well over a year to realize that they were actually losing money on large customer deals. They were paying substantial commissions to sales representatives who had adroitly figured out how to profit personally, as their employers lost money on each contingent worker who was dispatched.

Managing Growth Profitably

Growing the firm sounds like an admirable goal. But growing the firm profitably presents significant challenges, especially in finances and leadership. The delay between paying contingent workers and being paid by customers creates special cash management challenges for staffing firms. Providing an increasing number of contingent workers to customers exacerbates this dynamic. Fortunately, specialized vendors have cropped up to serve staffing firms' need for financing, and some banks have come to trust the staffing industry enough to offer industry-specific services. Growing and managing branch offices requires planning and leadership. Failures in these areas can throttle a firm's profitability, damage its brand image, or even cause it to go under. In this section, we discuss cash management, financing, and planning and managing the growth of branches.

Cash management

Profitability doesn't matter if there is insufficient cash to pay contingent workers or critical vendors (such as phone, rent, payroll processing, and drug test providers). There's a good reason for the expression "cash is king." Without it, your business will quickly go under.

In some businesses, money is collected before services are performed. Think of a magazine subscription, for example. You pay for a year's worth of issues, and a few weeks later they start arriving in your mailbox. But not so with staffing. Here, the inexorable weekly payroll is due immediately to your employees, while payment is typically received in 15 to 35 days (the average days outstanding for staffing companies is around 26).

Competitive staffing firms plan for this increasing short-term cash need and make sure that they have adequate cash on hand for all payroll-related expenses each week — that is the first rule of staffing cash management.

One common solution to the payroll cash flow challenge is to use external financial resources to cover any cash shortfall in the pay-bill cycle. Financing can come from banks, from general "factors" (see the following section for an explanation of factors), or from industry-knowledgeable funding companies that will loan money to cover payroll and take your receivables as collateral. Some funders offer to handle all payroll process, while others limit their service to the financing aspect.

Financing: factors, banks and funding firms

Whether a firm is a struggling startup or an established, but fast-growing firm with annual growth at 25% or more, it will probably need to bring in financing somewhere along the way. Many staffing firms use factoring companies to provide bridge funding between the day that the staffing firm must pay its contingent workers and when the customer pays the staffing firm's invoice for those workers. The decision to bring in such financing calls for foresight and a solid analysis of the costs and benefits of that financing. Such decisions should be made with the help of professionals with the relevant expertise.

Factoring is defined as the sale of a company's accounts receivable invoices to a third party in order to obtain working cash. The process goes by many names — receivables factoring, invoice factoring, bill factoring, or funding — though some experts want to distinguish between "basic" factoring and a variety of more recently offered programs that are more involved.

The reason that factoring is so important in staffing has to do with the unique product that the staffing industry offers — business labor. Because states require by law that employees be paid regularly and on time, staffing firms are not able to stretch their payment terms as is often done in manufacturing, wholesale, or retail — where actual inventory can be used as loan collateral. And when staffing firms are rapidly expanding, even a strong cash flow may not keep up with payroll requirements (see more on this in the Cash Management section later in this chapter).

In the most basic factoring relationship, the staffing company sells its invoices at a discount to the factor, which then charges back to the staffing firm any of them that remain unpaid. Typically they will lend between 80% and 90% of receivable value, which is more than adequate to cover payroll and burden. The factor often requires that its own company name or invoice be used, and that the staffing company's invoices are marked to indicate that the invoice is "owned" by the factor. Most staffing firms prefer to avoid this type of factoring, because their customers are made aware that their payables are being carried by a third party, and this is thought to create a bad image for the staffing company.

If a staffing firm's receivables are purchased "without recourse," the factoring firm does the collections; this is more often the case where the staffing firm has lost its collections ability. More typically, though, they are bought "with recourse," and the staffing firm will still be involved in collections efforts. One advantage to this type of basic factoring is that it may easily be used just for a short period of time, or with only certain invoices, and does not require the longer-term contract associated with more complex funding options.

Thirty years ago, financing options for staffing firms were primarily limited to choosing from one of the many generalist factoring firms, and the use of factors was less common. Today the alternatives are much more varied and industry-tailored, with many types of accounts receivable-based lending available to staffing owners, and financing companies much more prevalent in the staffing industry.

An alternative approach that has gotten traction in staffing is the provision by factors of invoicing services, or even of the entire payroll/ invoice processing function for the staffing firms it works with. In these arrangements — often called "funding services" — the factor may print and mail invoices and/or offer the direct funding for checks, all using the staffing firm's paper stock. Other funding firms may simply offer a line of credit to their business customers, using receivables as the collateral. Fees will vary based on the extent of services provided, and usually fall in the 1.0% to 6.0% range.

At the most service-intense end of the spectrum are full-service funding firms, which provide outsourced services for virtually all back-office functions for the staffing company and also provide operational advice, produce financial reports, supply business forms, and offer training resources. These factors operate somewhat like a franchisor, but allow the staffing firm to retain its unique brand name.

More recently, Web-based applications providers have also entered this "full service" market, even offering workers' compensation and risk management services to its customers. Some of these offerings also offer monthly fee programs rather than 12- to 24-month contracts.

As the staffing industry has grown, and funding has become more mainstream, competition for business has increased. Most factoring firms in the United States do at least some staffing firm business, and there are approximately 50 such firms that focus specifically on the staffing industry. As a result of this proliferation, the interest rates charged for funding have generally come down, while at the same time we've seen the addition of extra services and industry-specific products introduced by financial firms looking for a market advantage.

After factoring firms demonstrated that staffing firms can provide reliable business for those who offer financing, regional banks began entering this market, either by adding a factoring product for staffing firms to their portfolio of services, or by acquiring a funding company already serving the market. They found that staffing firm customers are generally good payers, and the risks are generally low. However, some local banks may still not understand the staffing business enough to lend without a personal guarantee from a small staffing firm's top management.

Funding firms that focus on the staffing industry remain the main source of lending to staffing vendors, and they can be found at almost every staffing industry trade show, association conference, and in trade magazines. Small staffing firms may be able to find a consultant who specializes in providing advice on financing. A small staffing firm's accountant may also be able to provide such advice, before the firm enters into any of these factoring or funding arrangements.

Adding services

Although we've seen a secular trend of increasing use of contingent and contract labor over the last few decades — and we expect to see that trend line pick up even more in the decades ahead — every experienced staffing firm operator is aware that the overall business cycle can dramatically affect the demand for, and supply of, contingent workers. It's best to plan market additions, office openings or new business lines to coincide with upward business cycle movements. Don't fight the market. It always wins!

These cycles tend to be even more pronounced in the permanent placement staffing sector, but the timing is not the same. While contingent worker hiring tends to drop early in a down cycle *and* come back early in up cycles, a reduction in permanent hires typically occurs later on in the down cycle, with renewed permanent hiring also delayed to later in the up-cycle. That said, it can be expedient to wait longer to hire on permanent placement consultants once an upturn in orders for contingent workers is underway, and to allow attrition or poor performance to reduce these positions internally once growth in contingent worker placement has plateaued. The addition of fees from permanent placements can boost a staffing firm's overall gross margins when hiring is strong (margins often can be around 50%), but keeping on too many permanent consultants through a year or more of weak hiring activity can have an equally negative impact on operating profit.

Temp-to-hire services (previously called "temp-to-perm" by many in our industry) can also increase gross margin. At first, this became well established in the commercial staffing segment, and has become increasingly used in the harder-to-fill professional skill categories. Staffing Industry Analysts estimates that about 7% of all reported temporary help sales in the United States in 2006 were the result of temp-to-hire placements.

Conversion from temporary to full-time regular payroll can be the result of a "try before you buy" strategy, where the customer brings on contingent workers with an intention of moving the "right" employee from temporary status to its own payroll. But it also can occur when the "chemistry" between employee and employer develops to the point where both become interested in a long-term relationship. In the try-before-you-buy scenario, customers tend to offer regular employment sooner rather than later, due to concerns that the employee may still look elsewhere for long-term employment.

Adding and managing branches

A significant majority of company employees work in locations away from headquarters — yet there is often relatively little attention paid to the successful management of these field operations. Other key relationships, such as between local branches, or between a branch or regional office and the company's headquarters functions and personnel, are often equally neglected. Applying the good habits identified in the six previous chapters will go a long way toward maintaining the business unit relationships and business results that you desire.

Take the simplest case: a one-office staffing firm that adds a new office. In staffing, as in many other businesses, the addition of a second office changes things dramatically. Adding a second office outside of the original metro area is even more complex. The branch office only needs to cover a few of the functions handled by the main office. Determining which functions to replicate requires some planning. Some staffing firms find that they need to expand with recruiting offices as their customer base grows, and a few — especially the professional areas (travel nurses or IT developers, for example) — are able to handle business that is national in scope from a single office or just a few regional locations. Nevertheless, most larger staffing firms today find that to service typical national industrial, office, or per diem medical business, it is preferable to have soldiers on the ground in a large number of metropolitan locations.

Just how many branches per metro area is another question altogether. Beware of being talked into opening branches unnecessarily just to satisfy egos or build empires. In our experience, larger offices tend to generate more excitement and reinforcement, and generally have greater productivity. New customers or recruiting requirements may provide a good reason to add an additional office, nevertheless.

It is best to be conservative in estimating office space requirements. In our experience, a small branch has typically needed between 800 and 1,200 square feet. Don't get saddled by overhead you don't need.

Most companies prefer to open a cluster of offices in a single metropolitan area with an area manager responsible for the cluster. Opening offices in the 10 largest cities may seem like the quickest way to put the largest number of temps to work, but the span of control for a single manager will be daunting. In other words, a manager can handle only so many direct reports before becoming stretched too thin to provide the support they need. The early months of a new office are exactly the time when its leader needs a lot of support. A sudden growth spurt that stretches the staffing firm's leadership resources can destroy its profitability.

Adding branches has pros and cons. Branches provide some economy of scale, as shared functions centralized at a main office reduce duplication. This enables a branch to bring in revenue without adding as much overhead cost as a standalone branch. Remote branches also allow a staffing firm to better serve customers with far-flung operations. As the Web continues to advance in sophistication, shared costs will be driven down even further.

These economies of scale make acquisitions or mergers more attractive. That is because already profitable branches can be combined to raise operating profits even further, while the firm gains offices in new locations without the usual ramp-up time and cost.

But, be careful, the "Starbucks model" doesn't generally work for staffing firms! Adding branches profitably can be very challenging. New branches typically take from one to two years to become profitable, although some — especially if started with a major customer in the bag — may be profitable right from the start. Others, despite all of your best efforts, may never manage to get out of the red. Realistically, founders and managers cannot count on each new branch to do as well, or start as fast, as that first or second office that they personally got up and running!

The same excellent service and consistent products makes Starbucks attractive to its customers. This is quite challenging for staffing firms — or any other service industry — to execute. What gives the firm its competitive advantage needs to be replicated in each branch office. That means instilling the company culture into each branch — its best practices in leadership, financial discipline, and core business processes such as targeting, acquiring, serving, and holding onto customers. Otherwise, each branch office becomes its own independent staffing firm, some operating profitably and others stumbling and perhaps even hurting the firm's brand image.

Two approaches work well for replicating best practices, and both can be used at the same time. One is role-modeling. For instance, management trainees, managers or supervisors at branch offices can work temporarily at an office where those best practices are part of everyday life. Another is documenting those best practices and using training and coaching to replicate them in each branch. Process mapping can be used to identify and standardize business processes that drive the firm's competitive advantage. Sometimes, entrepreneurs who start successful staffing firms know what to do, but find it hard to describe in ways that people new to the company can understand. In this case, an internal or external consultant can interview and shadow the successful entrepreneur and document what they do that works so effectively.

In the end, staffing is still a local business — never better than the local branch and its staff and management. Before expanding, staffing firm management needs to align its expansion plans with strategic reasons for expansion and examine its capacity to lead new branches. With planning and leadership of the kind described here, a staffing firm can expand profitably and build its brand.

Matching effort to pricing

The key to bottom line success is developing and maintaining a gap between what customers pay and what the staffing firm spends. It is <u>not</u> providing the best candidates — and the best service — in the world. Make sure your staff knows that the object of their efforts is <u>not</u> to wait until you have the best possible match for every temporary order that you are asked to fill. Rather, the object is to fill as many orders as possible, as quickly as possible, while maintaining acceptable quality standards — *as determined by your customer* (not your staff). If your office is working on direct hire orders, the object is to find an *acceptable* candidate who meets your customer's expectations, at the specified compensation level — not the one and only perfect candidate for the job!

The point is that whether it's sales or service, the time devoted to each customer must be commensurate with the margin dollars you expect to gain from their business. Filling just a few orders very well, or taking the time to locate the "perfect match" may sound like a great goal for your office or business, but it's not likely to be financially rewarding, except where the customer is willing to pay for such perfection. That's because it's unlikely that you can pass on the full costs of being excellent at a competitive rate. To bring dollars to the bottom line, you'll need to match the effort and cost expended for a customer to the bill rate that it will accept, and to the volume of business that it is offering.

Further, it's important that you set objectives for each type of staffing business you will take. If your customer requires that resumes be sent, backgrounds be checked, orientation or training videos be watched, or even that applicants be interviewed prior to starting assignments, fine — as long as your bill rate reflects your efforts and costs to provide these and other high-end services.

Even in a general clerical or industrial-only staffing branch office, customer expectations for their contingent workers range from "good enough" to "only the best." The key to developing these customers successfully is to set your sales and service levels to so that you can make a profit. Limit discounting to situations where there's a large enough volume or assignment duration that allows you to fill the order at a lower cost.

Designing and Outsourcing Non-core Processes

In the past two decades, companies have made great strides in profitability and implementing new strategies through process redesign and bringing in vendors to handle non-core processes. In this section, we explore some basics about payroll and collections processes, vendor selection for bringing in technology to support the firm's business processes or outsourcing the non-core processes entirely, and gaining access to templates and standard legal forms.

The pay-and-bill process

Two mundane but key functions for any staffing firm are payroll and invoicing. With some attention, they should stay mundane. Having a reliable, comprehensive, accurate, and user-friendly process for handling these two key financial functions plays an important role in creating confidence among contingent workers and customers. On the other hand, a single major error may put a firm out of business!

Billing timeliness and accuracy are important drivers of customer satisfaction. So, too, are on-time pay checks. Contingent workers who do not receive accurate checks each week are not very likely to stick around. And customers who can't routinely pay your invoices due to inaccuracies or process errors will quickly leave a deficit in your bank account — if not leave for another supplier as well! Both of these functions, payroll and billing, must work without fail. There is little tolerance for error.

Custom billing can net you additional business, but it may also clog up your process. Not only does it incur additional costs, customization also requires more time and attention, and often some additional software programming. It makes sense, therefore, that it should command a higher bill rate and probably also a minimum contract period commitment.

A similar caveat applies to electronic data exchange (EDE): Customers may ask for EDE if a firm does not already have it, but — as with custom billing — the firm must research what it will cost in additional staff, time, fees, equipment, and software. In either case, management should determine whether the firm's culture and competencies will support customization or electronic data exchange. If not, management can investigate what it would take to outsource it.

As your staffing firm grows, the ability to scale a payroll system (multiple states or countries, for example, or additional fields for new skill or assignment parameters) will become more important. A system that is built to handle payroll in just one jurisdiction may be easy or impossible to modify, depending on how it was first developed. An unexpected acquisition or merger may require integration of two dissimilar payroll processes, so in such circumstances be sure to investigate which system will be easier to modify, as well as which has the greatest scaling potential.

As we offered in Chapter 5, Exploiting Technology, there are many technical innovations in the payroll and billing areas. Outsourced application service providers (ASPs) now offer products that handle the pay-and-bill process along with many other staffing firm functions, such as risk management, funding, and front-office systems. Be sure to explore timecard scanning, electronic time clocks, online hours input, direct deposit, and the use of pay cards to replace checks, especially for blue collar workers.

Consider Paycards

Some 18% of *documented* workers (about 25 million employees) have no checking or bank accounts. Weigh the savings to these temporaries — no check cashing fee, and no travel to the office to pick up a check — against any new employee fees that will be charged by the pay card vendor. Some pay card vendors offer a range of additional benefits to your employees, which can be an additional retention feature. Keeping employees on the job Friday afternoons, and eliminating your own payroll processing costs, are additional benefits that you'll want to weigh in making a decision about pay cards.

Pay & Bill Rates

At some companies, the bill rate may be set first in the field by the sales force or management, or it may be stipulated in a contract, leaving it to the inside staff to try to maintain a profitable spread by adjusting the pay rate to a specific markup. For non-contract retail orders called in to the desk, a staffing rep may first search for an available candidate, then mark up their pay rate to get a bill rate. Either way, it often falls to the inside staff to produce a sufficient spread to make an adequate profit. Branch managers need to ensure that their sales and desk staff are always in sync regarding how an adequate spread will be maintained.

While high gross margin percentages are nice to have, you can't spend a percentage. It takes gross margin dollars to do that, and the way you get significant gross margin dollars is to combine a high bill rate with a high gross margin percentage. The lure of this combination is often what drives staffing owners to develop niche businesses with professional level skills.

IT staffing and travel nursing continue to offer high bill rates, typically exceeding $50 per hour (in 2009 dollars). On the other hand, legal, technical/engineering and other healthcare niches often exceed $30 per hour in bill rates. Of the professional segments, only finance and accounting fall below $30 an hour, most likely due to many companies including accounting clerks in this market segment. The traditional commercial staffing segments of office/clerical and industrial staffing offer bill rates averaging $18 and $14 respectively.

To remain competitive in your market — that is, with rates for services commensurate with other staffing providers competing for the same customers — you'll need periodic market research to understand what pay rates your temporary employees are being offered elsewhere, and what bill rates your customers are being asked to pay for various types of service and skills. Much of this intelligence can be gained through applicant interviews and visits to your temporaries on the job, or through sales visits and lunches with prospects and good customers.

Credit checking and collections

The need for collections is usually a result of the failure of credit-checking. Checking the credit score of new customers, and researching their capacity to make timely payments, is an important, and all-too-often neglected, part of the sales/service process. Ideally, credit-worthiness should be tested before an initial assignment begins, and then again periodically as the business relationship grows and the size of customer invoices increases. Typically, each account should be assigned a maximum outstanding balance amount based on credit-worthiness.

Find out if the customer has hired contingent workers recently billed through another service. Occasionally a company short on cash will stretch one staffing company to the limit, and then just move on to call another victim out of the blue. Beware of unexpectedly large orders that come in without any sales effort from your firm. Some staffing firms are reticent to take business from certain types of customers. Sole practitioner attorneys and politicians running for office come to mind.

A clear early warning signal of potential credit problems is a noticeable lengthening of the time taken by a customer to pay its bills, as measured in days sales outstanding (DSO). Competitive staffing firms negotiate the number of days within which the customer will pay (usually 30 days) and regularly check their accounting software reports for invoices that have not been paid in more than 30 days. They inquire with customers about any delay beyond the agreed-upon timeline and consider the need to stop service if the account is not made current. Because stopping service may be the basis for litigation, be sure to check with your attorney before taking this step.

Some staffing managers may worry that inquiring with the customer as the payment schedule has been reached will make the customer feel pressured. Instead, customers who experience the staffing firm as keeping its agreements and expecting the customer to do the same usually feel increased respect for what the staffing firm stands for. At times, delays are due to an accounting inaccuracy, a missing number on the staffing firm's invoice, or a process error either at the customer or at the staffing firm. Waiting beyond 30 days to find out about such errors obviously increases the difficulty of identifying the cause. Paper records get lost or stored away, recollection of events deteriorates, and the contingent worker (or even his/her customer supervisor) may have already moved on. Your accounting software should be able to help remind you at critical points in the billing cycle, producing an A/R schedule that shows which invoices are current and which are overdue 30, 60, and 90 days.

In cases where a customer is unable to pay for past services, early intervention is also critical. If a staffing firm's contingent workers are still being paid to work at the customer company, the firm continues to lose money. Also, waiting until the customer no longer needs the contingent workers removes some of the staffing firm's leverage to get a foot-dragging customer to pay.

Profitable staffing firms designate staff to review the A/R balances weekly, to make inquiry calls with customers, to collect payment for services on schedule, and to keep records of the inquiry calls, the customer's promises, and the extent to which the customer fulfilled on them. Such staff are given a simple process to raise red flags quickly to staffing firm management when A/R problems arise that represent significant potential losses. When customers run delinquent on sizeable sums, staffing firm managers make strategic decisions to remove contingent workers from a customer site and/or hire a collections firm to raise the stakes for delinquent customers who don't intend to keep their promise to pay.

As we discussed in the Chapter 5, technology can help staffing firms reduce costs by automating repeated processes. Automated call systems, online applications or scanned resumes, online testing tools, electronic payroll entry, and much more can dramatically increase the output of each person in your firm, thus requiring fewer employees and reducing labor costs. However, poorly planned or improperly implemented technology can be worse than keeping the status quo.

Effective vendor selection

There were more than 150 vendor exhibitors at the most recent American Staffing Association (ASA) exposition, offering a dizzying array of products and services to help staffing firms. Even the most experienced staffer there faced a mind-boggling range of options in dozens of product categories. Today, vendors are ready to help staffing firms with everything from risk management to information technology and assessment capabilities, just to name a few. Determining which tasks call for outside vendors, and then selecting from the many available, requires a lot of information and a good picture of how the firm operates and should be operating.

Selecting a front- and back-office software provider can be the most complex of all vendor selection processes for a staffing firm executive. The first step is to map the current business processes and then to envision how processes ought to be done in the future. It's virtually impossible to implement every best practice or desired feature at the same time (due to financial or space or time or staff constraints, just for example), so there are often important trade-offs or priority decisions that management and knowledgeable employees must make. As we mentioned earlier, process mapping and discussions about ideal future processes open up debates about how the operation should be run. And vendors sometimes lose patience with customer firms that have trouble determining what processes they want the software to support.

The next step is determining which software features, functions, and interfaces will best support the staffing firm's processes. That review often requires a team effort to set priorities for which functionality is a must-have and which is nice to have. Management must decide what the staffing firm can afford.

After setting priorities for software functionality and determining a budget, the staffing firm identifies staffing industry vendors that can meet its needs within the budget. There are many resources available for locating potential solutions. Staffing Industry Analysts' *SI Review* magazine, for example, lists and compares 32 back-office staffing software vendors in its May 2008 issue, focusing on more than a dozen specific system characteristics. Even more software providers are listed in *SI Review*'s annual "Buyers Guide," which is part of every January issue of *SI Review*, and also online at www.staffingindustry.com.

If a staffing firm's needs are more immediate, an even broader list of front- and back-office vendors (as well as information on more than 30 other categories of staffing products and services) is available at Staffing Industry Analysts' online *Supplier Directory* Web page, along with a way to contact them (www.staffingindustry.com).

A similar process can be used for other types of vendors: determining the staffing firm's needs and budget and locating vendors that can meet those needs within the available budget. Regardless of the particular product or service being evaluated, staffing firm leaders will want to consider asking vendors for (a) references to customers using or transitioning from something similar, (b) referrals from trusted peers in the industry, and

(c) a demonstration of how the product or service actually performs in the staffing firm's environment or with its processes. Leaders may also seek the help of unbiased industry consultants with expertise and experience. It is not advisable to settle for vendor-supplied references or "canned" demonstrations on a trade show floor, although those sources can provide some useful information when asked probing questions.

In addition to the specific features of the product or service that the staffing firm's team have deemed critical, it is worth investigating additional vendor attributes, as well; these include track records on ease of working with the vendor's product or service, quality of service, speed in responding to issues and special requests, customer mix, extent of lost business, as well quality and timeliness of software updates. The ability to scale and upgrade with ease is also important for many types of products.

Before signing on the dotted line, the staffing firm will want to carefully read the vendor's service-level agreement and any other legal documents that need to be signed. Look carefully at provisions for emergency service, routine maintenance, initial and ongoing vendor training, installation timeline, warranty, and customer responsibilities. For most vendor contracts, the firm will also want to get the advice of a business attorney.

Orchestrating Growth for Your Business or Branch

As we said at the start, most successful staffing suppliers will have a competitive advantage in at least a few of the seven key areas we have covered. It's unlikely that any one business or branch will have it all. The key to success is *continuous work* at developing leadership skills, people and culture management, building internal and external relationships, managing risk and profitability, and mastering technology. Growing a business, or a branch, requires continuous attention to all of these seven areas.

In companies with multiple branches or markets, the acceptable level of growth for a branch office is best determined in conjunction with higher-level management. It is likely to depend to a great degree on where the branch is in its life cycle: just opened with a year or two under its belt, or already a major profit producer for the firm.

For the staffing business as a whole, we find that owners often set very different goals for their business future. Some are content to reach a plateau where there is an adequate income stream for their family, and maybe something still left over to put away and invest for future years. This is understandable, but contains an element of risk, as changes come so fast today that it's easy to be overpowered by technical or competitive forces, whatever your business.

Looking at the broader marketplace, the U.S. labor force is projected to grow at just about one percent per year over the next decade, and GDP growth seems to range from one to three percent, depending on where we are in the business cycle. But, inflation may push costs up faster. And Staffing Industry Analysts forecasts that overall U.S. staffing revenue will grow at a 5% rate through 2016. That said, a five percent growth rate or better for your business might seem like a realistic goal for your staffing branch or firm.

We'd hope that by practicing the habits detailed in this volume, you could *double that growth* in your own staffing business. Indeed, an average annual growth rate of 15% seems to us well within reach of better operating staffing providers whenever the economy is not sliding into a recession. In the July 2008 issue of its *Staffing Industry Report* newsletter, Staffing Industry Analysts listed 61 smaller staffing firms that have averaged 25% growth or better over the years 2003-2007. And a few of them have kept up this pace for a decade or more! SIA calls these top performers "The 25% Club."

How do they do it? We'd like to think it's a function of applying the seven attributes of highly competitive staffing firms that we have outlined for you in this book. We won't say it's easy, but we hope that you will join them before too long!

References and Suggested Reading

Anastasi, Anne. 1988. *Psychological Testing, 6th ed.* New York: Macmillan. 28.

Bridges, William. 1991. *Managing Transitions: Making the most of change.* Reading, Mass.: Addison-Wesley.

Collins, Jim. 2001. *Good to Great.* New York: HarperCollins.

Cummings, T. G. & Worley, C. G. 2005. *Organization Development and Change, 8th ed.* Mason, OH: Thomson South-Western.

Finkelman, Jay. 2005. "A Focus on 10 Years," *Staffing Industry Review* (December).

Gibb, Jack. 1995. "Defensive Communication," in D. Kolb, J. Osland, & I Rubin (Eds.), *The Organizational Behavior Reader.* NJ: Prentice-Hall. 24-229.

Greble, T. C. & Kirsh, R. L. 2002. "Beware of the Temporary Trap: The Application of EEO Laws to Staffing Firm Employees." Retrieved on June 24, 2004, from http://www.shrm.org/hrresources/lrpt_published/CMS_000978.asp.

Harvey, Jerry B. 1988. The Abilene Paradox and other meditations on management. San Diego: University Associates.

Kirkpatrick, D. L. 1959. Techniques for evaluating training programs. *Journal of the American Society of Training and Development.* 13:3-9.

Lopez, Tará Burnthorne, Christopher D. Hopkins, and Mary Anne Raymond. 2006. "Reward Preferences of Salespeople: How Do Commissions Rate?" *Journal of Personal Selling & Sales Management.* (26) 4:381-390.

Nielsen, J. 2005. "Human Resources Management Comes of Age in the Courtroom: California Formally Enshrines the Importance of Human Resources Expert Testimony for Employment Litigation," *The Psychologist-Manager Journal* (8)2:157-164.

Noe, Raymond A. 2008. *Employee Training and Development, 4th ed.* New York: McGraw-Hill.

Phillips, Jack J. (2003). *Return on Investment in Training and Performance Improvement Programs, Second Edition (Improving Human Performance)*. New York: Butterworth-Heinemann.

Weick, Karl E. 2001. *Making Sense of the Organization*. Malden, MA: Blackwell Publishers.

Equal Opportunity Employment Commission, "Federal Laws Prohibiting Job Discrimination Questions and Answers," www.eeoc.gov/facts/qanda.html

About the Authors

Jay M. Finkelman, Ph.D., C.P.E.

Jay M. Finkelman is system-wide associate dean, professor and program director of Alliant International University's Marshall Goldsmith School of Management (MGSM), Organizational Psychology Division. He served as a senior manager, consultant and expert witness in employment, staffing and human resources management for over two decades. He has had hundreds of retentions and depositions, and testified at trial 42 times.

Dr. Finkelman is an industrial and forensic psychologist as well as a certified professional ergonomist. He holds a Ph.D. in industrial-organizational psychology from New York University and an MBA in industrial psychology from the Bernard M. Baruch School of Business of The City College of The City University of New York. He was a tenured full professor of industrial psychology at The City University of New York (CUNY) as well as dean of students at Baruch College. He also served on the doctoral faculty in business, specializing in organizational behavior, at the Graduate Center of CUNY.

Dr. Finkelman served in a variety of senior line management positions after leaving CUNY, including station manager of KTVU Television Channel 2 in San Francisco, vice president in charge of marketing for Walt Disney television, and senior vice president and general manager for Kelly Services in the human resources management and staffing industry.

Dr. Finkelman holds a Diplomate from the American Board of Professional Psychology and from the American Board of Forensic Psychology, where he is also a fellow. He is a certified personnel consultant from the National Association of Personnel Consultants and a certified employment specialist from the California Association of Personnel Consultants. He is a licensed psychologist in the state of California and in the state of New York and is listed in the National Register of Health Service Providers in Psychology. He is a member of Psi Chi, Delta Sigma Rho – Tau Kappa Alpha and Beta Gamma Sigma, and received the Excellence in Teaching Award from CUNY.

He is a member of the Industrial Psychology and Engineering Psychology Divisions of the American Psychological Association, the Human Factors and

Ergonomics Society and the American Academy of Forensic Psychology. Dr. Finkelman specializes in human resources, staffing industry management practices, employment discrimination (gender, age, race, and disability), sexual harassment, Americans with Disabilities Act, compensation practices, wage & hours, independent contractor status, conflict of interest, negligent hiring/retention, wrongful termination, adverse impact, performance appraisal, psychometrics, statistical analysis, human factors and ergonomics.

Jonathan Troper, Ph.D.

Jonathan Troper is the director of the Center for Innovation and Change and assistant professor at the Marshall Goldsmith School of Management at Alliant International University, where he teaches industrial-organizational psychology at the masters and doctoral levels. He has served in a variety of positions ranging from executive recruiter to staff director in for-profit and not-for-profit organizations. He has authored several publications and taught at the University of Southern California.

Dr. Troper earned his Ph.D. from UCLA in psychological studies in education, with research and coursework at the Anderson Graduate School of Management. He also holds a bachelors degree from Amherst College.

Dr. Troper has led many organizational consulting projects involving leadership development, organizational change, communication planning, employee surveys, training evaluation, management and executive coaching. He is certified in the Personnel Decisions International PROFILOR® 360-degree assessment and feedback coaching for managers and executives.

Dr. Troper is co-chair of the Organization Development Special Division of the American Society for Training and Development Los Angeles Chapter, and is a member of the Society of Industrial-Organizational Psychology and the Society for Human Resource Management.